You Don't Remember. I Can't Forget

By

Anna Pinack-Carrabs

Anna Pinack Carrabs

You Don't Remember– I can't Forget

Mass Paperback Printing April 2008

ISBN 978-0-9809075-6-0

www.bestbookpublish.com

Best Book Publish

First electronic printing October 2007

ISBN 978-0-9784265-4-5

Chapter 1

I was born in the summer of 1947; the first-born. My mother was just seventeen and my father was twenty-two years old. I grew up in an area of Toronto known as Cabbage Town, Mutual and Gerrard Streets. My step grandfather, Colin, but everyone called him Uncle Joe? He owned the house, and it was a big three-story red brick building. He lived on the first floor with my maternal grandmother (this was her second marriage) and we lived on the second floor. My aunt, Karen, and uncle Kevin, lived in the attic. When you came in the front door, the hallway was divided in two. A wooden staircase went straight up to the second floor. The hallway next to it led to my uncle Joe's place. The living room was huge; it was dull and dingy looking, because the windows faced the brick wall of the house next door. The table and chairs were old and made of solid maple, but the red velvet couch was so comfortable that one wanted to cuddle up into. The kitchen next to the living room was big, but it was nice and bright. The back door led to a small porch and a backyard. As you made your way back to the hallway, there was another door, which led to their front room that faced the street and was a combination bedroom and sitting room. It always smelled musty.

We lived on the second floor, and as you came up the stairs there was a small square landing. Then three small steps that led down a long hallway. To your right was the kitchen and it was small. The table, which only had room for three chairs, was right near the window. With the refrigerator and stove at the opposite end, there wasn't much room left to move around. The bathroom was right next-door and it was the size of the master bedroom. The bathtub had legs with ornamental designs on them and in one corner stood an old ringer washing machine. At the end of the hall was my uncle David's, (my mother's brother's) room. As you made your way back to the landing next to the stairs, there were three small steps going to the left. That's where the bedrooms were. The first door on the left was my bedroom. There was only one window in my room and when you opened it you could see the back yard and the laneway. There was a small wooden ledge about three feet square, on which mom would set the basket of laundry down and hang the clothes on the line to dry.

Next to my room was a staircase leading up to the attic. Another door next to that staircase led to a large front room. This was my parents' bedroom that doubled as our living room. We only had two rooms.

The staircase that I mentioned earlier led up to the attic. My aunt Karen, (my mother's sister) and uncle lived up there. At the top of the stairs to the right of another small landing was a large bedroom that doubled as their living room. The sparsely furnished room was dark. To the left of the landing was another room, which was a combination kitchen/dining room. It was much brighter and the door led onto the roof, which I thought was so cool. Of course, being the only kid in the house, I did receive a lot of attention, until 1949, when my brother Barry was born. There were a lot of kids in the neighborhood to play with. We played hopscotch and tag in a vacant lot beside one of the houses. There were numerous laneways in the neighborhood too, where we played hide and seek. I felt safe and loved very much until something happened that changed my entire life.

It was the summer of 1952 and I was five years old and now had two younger brothers. Barry and Gary. My brother Barry, who was three years old, was trying to carry his tricycle up the stairs and he was having a hard time. I was standing on the third step from the bottom, when he turned to me and asked me to help him. I said, 'no' and he moved towards me and pushed me. I fell backwards and landed at the bottom of the stairs. The pain I felt was incredible. I started screaming and screaming that I can't move. Then someone came and picked me up. That's when I lost consciousness. *Even though what Barry did was terrible, it saved my life, because no one had any idea that I was sick.*

I woke up feeling very groggy. The light blinded my eyes and there were a lot of people, wearing white coats, just staring down at me. *Why can't I move? Where am I? This could not be happening to me! It must be a dream! Where is mommy? What are these people in white coats going to do to me? I want to go home.*

I remember getting a needle and falling asleep. This time when I awoke, I felt tightness around my body and struggled to move, but I couldn't. This was my first cast, which was fitted from my armpits to just above my bum. I felt so confined and helpless. Being fed and changed was also very humiliating. *I'm five years old. What is happening to me?*

My condition was very serious, because I was not getting better. As a result of the fall, my spine was crushed at T12. This condition, that affects the upper back, which controls the signals to the chest muscles, some of the back muscles and parts of the abdomen, left the doctors no alternative but to operate. A decision was made to take a piece of my collarbone and fuse it into the injured area.

I really had no recollection of how long I had this cast on, or how it was taken off. What I do remember was the day the nurse came and helped me into a wheelchair. My mother walked beside us as the nurse wheeled me to a large brightly lit room. It reminded me of a school gym.

I really felt frightened as I noticed several white coats sitting to one side of the room. My mother was sitting beside me until the nurse wheeled me into the center of the room and left me there. One of the white coats instructed me to stand up and walk to the other end of the room. As I stood up, all eyes were upon me and I felt that I was on display. After taking a couple of steps, I suddenly feel a jolt of pain at the top of both my legs. I was in pain, but I kept going. All of a sudden I started to wobble from side to side. The pain became so intense that I collapsed and lost consciousness. This was not good. *I am not getting better and no one has any answers.*

You Don't Remember– I can't Forget

My parents started to look around and found a white coat that had a small practice at College and Spadina. He diagnosed me as having Histiocytosis. A generic term that refers to an increase in the number of Histiocytosis, a type of white blood cell, that act as scavengers to remove foreign material from the blood and tissues. Since recent research demonstrated Langerhan cell involvement as well as Histiocytosis, this led to a proposal that the term Langerhans Cell Histiocytosis (LCH) be used in place of Histiocytosis. Either term refers to three separate illnesses (listed in order of increasing severity) eosinophilic granuloma, Hand-Schuller-Christain disease and Letterer-Siwe disease. I had the second form, Hand-Schiller Christen Disease, a chronic scattered form of Histiocytosis. It occurs most commonly from the age of one to three years and is a slow progressive disease that affects the softened areas of the skull, other flat bones, the eyes, and skin.

By the time it was ascertained that a child had this disease it was too late. The children would die at puberty. No one as young as me had ever been diagnosed with this disorder, so there was hope. My parents signed all the forms to proceed with medical intervention.

Chapter 2

When I woke up mom was there with a nurse. I noticed other beds in the room, but they were all empty and I could hear talking and laughter coming from somewhere down the hallway. The nurse asked me if I would like to join the other children. Without a word, mom turned around and walked away. I felt abandoned. I screamed and screamed until everything went blank. *She can't leave me.*

I have vague memories of being given a regimen of needles and oral medications. Of being wheeled into rooms where big machines were suspended from the ceiling. Lying on cold metal tables and this white coat manipulating my body. I have little recollection of what was going on at that time. The drugs, along with those big machines, made me feel sick and very weak.

My father would become very emotional when I recall the times that he would come to see me in the hospital. He never knew what to expect. One day I would be as red as a tomato, or covered in orange dots. His ruminating surprised me, because I had a hard time remembering him coming to see me at all.

What I do remember is the day a white coat came into my room with a wheelchair. I was helped into the chair and I immediately flashed back to that one day when I attempted to walk and collapsed. I felt nervous as if something awful was going to happen to me. This room was different from the last one and was nice and bright. There were other patients in the room and they were busy doing all types of activities. I was wheeled in front of a long plank with railings on each side. The white coat helped me stand and instructed me to hold onto the railings. Then I was told to walk to the other end. This was the beginning of my physiotherapy.

After a week or so I was able to give up the wheelchair and walk on my own without any help or support. I felt good, not sick at all and started to ask if I could go home. Arrangements were made and by the weekend I went home. I was so excited. I couldn't wait to see my brothers. However, when that day arrived the unthinkable happened. Without any explanation this white coat lifted me onto a backboard with a hump in the middle. He didn't say a word as he strapped me in nice and tight. I could not move at all and felt like I was being punished. Being restrained is a terrible feeling. *What is wrong with me?*

The trip home was by ambulance and mom was beside me. When we arrived, there were a lot of people standing around nodding and looking sad. I felt like I was on display and very self-conscious. I remember being carried upstairs to my room on the second floor, but cannot recall seeing my brothers anywhere. *Being fed and changed was humiliating. I'm five years old.*

At night I could hear muffled voices of people talking and arguing, which interrupted my sleep. This was so different from the hospital. I didn't feel safe at all and when it was time for me to return to the hospital, I was carried down the stairs headfirst. I was terrified and thought I was going to slide out and fall on my head. I was so scared and began to wonder if I really mattered. The visit home was not good, and back in the hospital I felt safe. Here they knew how to handle me. It was early in the morning and I could hear the white coats marching down the hall. I started to feel uneasy. What were they going to do to me this time? They stood around the bed and one of them spoke about the ongoing procedures regarding my condition. *What is wrong with me?*

Christmas was not far away and there was a lot of excitement in the air. My friends and I must have made quite a ruckus, pushing and shoving each other, vying for window space to get a glimpse of the Santa Claus, as he came to visit us.

We had a lot of fun and I was thrilled because the following day I was going home for the Christmas Holidays. Mom helped me to get dressed and as she gathered up my belongings the nurse entered the room with a wheelchair. My mind started racing; *if I can walk now why do I need this chair?*

I was so happy as I said goodbye to all the friends that I had made during my stay. As she wheeled me to the elevator I felt anxious and confused. I wondered, would I ever see them again. My thoughts began to wonder; maybe I'm just being moved to another room, but when the elevator door opened and I could see the street through the glass doors, I breathed a sigh of relief.

I was very excited as I stood up and took my mother's hand as we left the hospital. It was cold outside, but I could walk and felt so independent. *I can't wait to see my brothers and I miss my nana too.*

It was summer when I had my accident and now it was winter. I must have been in the hospital for at least six months. Even though I was excited about going home and seeing my brothers, I couldn't help thinking of my last visit there; being restrained and carried downstairs head first. But this time it was different. I was not restrained and felt much better. I asked mom if I had to go back to the hospital and she told me that I would still have to go to the clinic for check ups, but now only as an outpatient. *The dreaded waiting rooms; sitting there listening to the other patients crying and moaning did not help. I'm feeling anxious and my mind is racing. What are the white coats doing to them, because I knew that sooner or later I could be next?*

Chapter Three

When we arrived home I was a little disoriented. The house looked the same. The same people lived there, but something was different. There were a lot of people standing on the sidewalk nodding and looking at me. *What is wrong with me?*

I felt so independent because I could walk, but I became unsure of myself as I stared at the veranda steps. This was new to me and I felt a bit uneasy. There were no stairs in the hospital. Dad carried me up onto the landing and as I walked into the house I could see the stairs leading up to the second floor. Now I became paralyzed with fear and backed away. I didn't want to go near them. My mind immediately flashed back to the accident, and I could clearly see myself lying at the bottom of the stairs; screaming. I think I blacked out, because I can't remember too much after that.

Christmas came and went. I don't remember too much about it, because I was overwhelmed with everything. When I went into the hospital it was summer and when I came home it was Christmas. I felt different, like a stranger and had to familiarize myself with everything and everyone. We lived on the second floor, so I had little choice, but to confront my fear of the stairs. Going up was not too bad, even though I was very apprehensive. Standing at the top of any stairs and looking down is still terrifying. This would become the most formidable task of my life, because there are stairs everywhere.

As I mentioned earlier my brothers and I shared a room. I slept on a cot beside the door, and they slept together in this huge square bed. What an adjustment this was for me, so different from the hospital. At night I had terrible dreams and would wake up screaming. Other times I could hear muffled sounds of people talking and arguing. Sometimes I was too afraid to even go to the bathroom, so wet myself. Then I would crawl into bed with my brothers. I'm sure they complained to mom and dad.

In June I turned six years of age. My oldest brother now four, the youngest was two and a half and in March we were all expecting a new baby brother or sister. *Mom certainly would have her hands full.*

When I returned to school I was still in grade one and filled with such curiosity. Physical activity of any kind was definitely a no, no. I couldn't understand why, because I was able walk. All I could do was to adjust and wonder why I'm treated differently than the other kids. *What is wrong with me?*

Earlier I mentioned that my step grandfather, or Uncle Joe, had more living space than anyone else in the house. I loved spending time with my nana (mother's mother, Elizabeth), and would sneak downstairs to be with her. She never treated me differently, especially not like some of their guests. On weekends everyone congregated there, especially in the evening. Some of the neighbors would drop by, but there were men and women who I can't remember, or have ever seen before coming and going from his place. They made a real fuss over me too, which I didn't really like. It was as if they all felt sorry for me. I didn't want that.

As the evening progressed, all the adults were drinking and started staggering around, and speaking real stupidly. I thought it was really funny. Then mom made me and my brothers go upstairs to bed.

Other times, when there was no school, we would all get in the car and visit dad's aunt Grace and uncle Daniel. They were Ukrainian and lived on a farm in Bowmanville, Ontario. It was a dairy farm with lots of cows and chickens. They had a son and a daughter much older than myself. They also had a big dog that growled too much and scared me a lot. Dad always brought along one of his rifles so he and his uncle could go into the fields hunting gophers. Dad's aunt was really nice, but she didn't speak English very well, but she and mom got along fine. While dad was gone we went out and explored the farm.

On the way to the barn you had to watch where you walked, because there was cow dung everywhere. The barn had a terrible smell to it. I think it was because it wasn't cleaned very often. We then investigated the chicken coop and helped ourselves to some eggs, which we took home with us. We learned how to milk cows, which was a lot of fun. What turned me off was after my brothers finished milking the cow, they would drink the milk right out of the bucket. Since then, I do not like milk at all. These outings were very important to me, because inside I felt different; it allowed me to bond with my family. I had been separated for quite awhile from my brothers and always felt like something was lacking in our relationship, so getting together like this was important. Just because I'm sick and disabled it shouldn't matter. *I don't know where I belong.*

There was no health care (OHIP) in place then, and dad was learning the painting business, so money was scarce. Nana would help us out sometimes. When there was no work dad played the horses, gambled and played pool to make ends meet. When dad had a few drinks in him he would reminisce about my hospital stays and this one-day when he came to see me in the hospital, someone from the Accounting Department informed him that he owed the hospital almost a thousand dollars. He did not have that kind of money and told them, "To keep me there." His comments made me feel like a burden on everyone, just worthless. I would cry myself to sleep. *His drinking scares me.*

There was a white coat that I saw a lot when I was in the hospital. He was personally involved in my case and suggested to parents that I stay with him for a while. He assured them that I would be well looked after, and there would be no cost involved.

My parents agreed and the debt my father owed the hospital was paid in full. However, I overhear dad becoming incessant about this white coat though, adamant that he was having an affair with a nurse. I had no idea what he was talking about. *His drinking starts to scare me.*

Chapter 4

I did indeed stay with this white coat, and it was during the summer holidays. I must have undergone very radical treatments because I can't remember anything about him. I was not conscious of where I lived either. To this day it is a creepy feeling not being able to remember that part of my life. He will always remain a mystery to me, and yet I think he is responsible for saving my life. What I do remember was the day my parents came to take me home.

It was a nice, sunny day as the white coat took my hand and led me out onto the front porch. The street below was so clean and there were lots of trees and flowers everywhere. There was a car parked across the street and I watched as my parents made their way towards us. *I feel a bit uneasy wondering what's going on.*

Mom was making a big fuss about the dress I was wearing as she took my hand. Dad was still talking to the white coat as mom and I walked to the car. *I'm feeling confused. Where do I belong?*
The familiar neighborhood came into view as I stared out of the car window on the way home. I could not control anything that was happening to me. The treatments and some oral medications didn't seem to end. I was still an outpatient. I looked forward to seeing my nana, but felt a bit apprehensive as I got out of the car and wondered if I was missed at all.

When I got back to school I entered Grade 2. I could walk, run and jump; however, physical activity was still a no, no. During recess I would just stand around more or less, feeling so different from the other kids. It was hard trying to make friends, connect, or just fit in. I was seven years old now. My oldest brother was five; the next one was three and a half and the youngest, a year old now. My aunt and uncle had their first baby and it was a girl. I was learning how to change diapers and having a lot of fun playing with her and my baby brother. Sometimes when I didn't have any school, my grandfather, would take me to work with him. He worked downtown in one of these old office/factory buildings, doing maintenance work. He also made sure the boilers were working properly. It was a quiet and spooky place and I was enthralled with the sounds of the creaking floors, and the smell of old wood. There were a few people working and they would give me paper to write on and let me play with some of the different office machines while my step grandfather was busy doing maintenance work. It was fun and I really enjoyed these outings very much.

My next outing was back to the Hospital. Even though mom was with me, I felt very nervous. We were taken to an examination room and this white coat took measurements of my body; from my armpits to my bum and that was it. Another appointment was made to see him again in a week. I felt confused as we made our way home.

When the time came to see this white coat I was uneasy, because I was not sure what to expect. When we arrived, he helped me put on a made-to-measure back brace. It had the same concept as a corset, though without the lace in the back. The shoulder straps were made of thick soft leather and the front was fitted with stiff leather and straps that tied up like shoelaces. The back of the brace had thick strips of solid steel embedded into the fabric. The brace felt cumbersome at first and the only time I was allowed to remove it was when I went to bed, or bathed. It helped me with my posture and gave my back very good support. I could now bend and twist my body just enough. So it wasn't too restrictive. I am really not sure how long I had to wear this brace. The best thing about it was, no one could tell I had it on. During the winter my mother put it into the oven to warm it up before I went to school.

Dad had a real appreciation for the great outdoors. As I said earlier, we would go and visit his aunt and uncle in Bowmanville. When we did not go to the farm, dad would take us to the provincial parks or just drive down some dirt roads. We had some great adventures, but I will never forget this one Saturday. Dad had found the perfect spot for a picnic, while driving down an old country road. Trees surrounded us and there was a small stream nearby. It was a peaceful scene, with the sun's warm rays glittering through the canopy above and down to the green grasses below. After we had lunch, dad took his rifle and wondered off into the woods all by himself. My brothers and I had a great time playing in the cool waters of the stream, catching frogs and exploring different plant life that grew along its banks. I always had to be careful not to get my brace wet.

It was starting to get dark and dad had been gone for a long time when mom suggested that we all get into the car, and wait for him there. As I sat in the back seat of the car watching the darkness envelope the car I had feelings of abandonment and was shaking with fear wondering if we would get home. Suddenly I saw a light flashing in the distance and breathed a sigh of relief, it was dad. He put the rifle into the trunk and then got behind the wheel and started heading home. After awhile it seemed as if we were going nowhere. My brothers and I sat quietly in the back seat and when I strained my neck to look out the window to see where we were going, it was pitch black, and all I could see absolutely nothing. I thought we were going to fall off a cliff and started screaming hysterically. My brothers must have thought I had gone crazy. *I have an overactive imagination.*

We live in a rough neighborhood and I think that these outings are dad's attempt at trying to keep us out of it as much as possible. For me it was an opportunity to feel a sense of belonging.

Chapter 5

It was 1955 and in June I turned eight years old, which meant summer holidays had arrived. I was finding school very difficult, with some of the subjects very hard to comprehend, and there never seemed to be any encouragement at home. The other students distracted me often. My medical issues did interfere with my education and socializing skills. With determination though, I managed to pass into Grade 3. I was really proud of myself.

Just as school ended and the summer holidays began, I had an appointment at the hospital. It was a different clinic that we went to this time. Mom helped me undress and put on the hospital gown. When we were finished, a nurse helped me into a wheelchair, which made me very nervous, because I could walk.

As we waited for the elevator I got a feeling that something awful was about to happen. As the door opens, we found ourselves in the basement. The walls were made of concrete blocks, and were gray in color. Really dingy looking. There was no one else around and the silence was deathly. Then the nurse wheeled me down the hallway, where we entered a room that really smelled awful. I was relieved that mom was with me. The room was small and windowless, but it had a bed, a few chairs. I noticed this long square knotted twine, which reminded me of a spider web, hanging from the ceiling. The white coat positioned me under it, took off my hospital gown and asked me to stand as straight as I could and hold onto the net. He started wrapping these cold and wet white strips of cloth around my body; first under my armpits, and almost down to my bum. I started to feel a tightness of the cloth engulf my body and at that moment realized I wasn't going home.

I was lifted onto a stretcher. I felt angry and insignificant. *No one ever explains things to me, so I can't help feeling betrayed.* I am taken to a different part of the hospital this time. The room had six beds, and the other kids are around my age. At least I'm not alone.

My spine was still weak and the bones were taking longer to heal so I still had needles and oral medications to contend with. The radiation treatments were the worst as they made me feel nauseous. I started to notice that my hair was getting thinner and falling out.

All that I was able to do was move my head up and down and from side to side, so I had to be fed and changed. I found this very humiliating. It didn't take long for me to ask the person, who was feeding me, to hand me the dish of jello that was on my tray. By resting the dish on top of my chest and lifting the spoon as close to my mouth as possible, I managed to finish it all. It was painful at first, but I persisted in feeding myself and after a week, I was able to finish everything on my tray. It wasn't long after that, that I was out of bed and mobile.

I felt so independent, but all of a sudden when I walked a short distance, the cast began to slip. I felt a jolt of pain in my back and had to hold the cast up as I walked. *I don't know who to go to for help.*

After a day or so, without any warning a white coat came into my room and sat me in a wheelchair. While we were waiting for the elevator I began to feel really uneasy again. The elevator stopped and we are in the basement. Now my mind really started to race. I'd probably have to have a new cast put on, or something awful was going to happen.

As we entered this room I had a flashback of having the first cast put on. I couldn't help feeling scared as the white coat positioned me over the net again, but I was relieved when he told me to just stay seated and relax. Without any explanation he imbedded these soft foamy leather shoulder straps right into the cast. The procedure did not take long at all and I was so relieved as I was wheeled me back to my room. *The ward I'm in is like a second home.*

The other kids were a comfort to me, because we were all going through the same thing. One day during lunch we were all laughing and joking around when this nurse, who was wearing a white coat, came over to my bed. She pointed her finger right at me and told me that eating with my mouth open was very rude. Then she took hold of the curtains and pulled them all around the bed. The feeling of isolation was overwhelming. I cried and cried. Being restrained is indeed a helpless feeling, but isolation is dreadful; nobody knows you are even there. I could not comprehend why this nurse was so mean to me. Now, whenever I saw her I felt ill at ease. What did I do? *What is wrong with me?*

It wasn't long after that incident that I was discharged from the hospital, and I couldn't believe it, because I still had the body cast on and was almost bald. I felt sad as I said good-bye to my friends, but I was happy to be going home and looked forward to seeing my nana. I thought about school too. When it was time to go back I'd be going into grade 4.

While I was in the hospital mom would bring me my schoolwork. There were many distractions and not much discipline; education was not the priority here. When we finally got home the whole neighborhood was there. I felt like I was on display, everyone was nodding and had a sad look on their faces. *I couldn't help but wonder what was wrong with me.*

The cast was really cumbersome and I was a little apprehensive as I walked up the veranda steps and into the house. I looked everywhere for my nana, but she was nowhere to be found. I was told that she had gotten sick and was taken away to the hospital. I never saw her again. She was 49 years old and had died of alcoholism. It is my first knowledge about death and loss.

I was in for a big surprise too. Arrangements had been made for my uncle (mother's brother) to move downstairs and look after his stepfather, who was 66 years of age. I inherited my uncle's room. It was a small dingy room. There was one window that faced the backyard and my bed was next to the door.

The weekends did not change much, except at night. People would drop by my grandfather's place. It was fun, until some people started staggering and couldn't talk properly. That's when mom would make us go upstairs into bed. Sometimes I woke up by the muffled sounds of people arguing. Even though I am closer to the bathroom there were times when I was afraid to get up. There is no one I could cuddle up to. My parents and brothers seemed so far away. I felt segregated at times. So different from the hospital; all the adults in the house would be drunk, except mom.

Chapter 6

When it was time to go to school I felt very apprehensive. The cast was heavy and was uncomfortable. I had to wear a hat, because my head was as bald as the day I was born. I didn't really want to be there, but mom reassured me that everything would be fine. After we found my classroom mom left, leaving me feeling abandoned as the teacher introduced me to the other students. Some of them snickered. Their reaction made me feel very self-conscious. I found a desk at the back of the classroom and settled into it so I could catch up.

I was relieved when I met a girl, Cheyenne, at school who had just moved into the neighborhood. Her house was up the street, right by the entrance to the laneway. She was the oldest of two brothers, where as I had three. Her grandmother and mother were Ojibwa Indians, and her father was French.

I introduced her to the other kids that I knew in the neighborhood, which for some reason didn't seem to go over so well. After awhile I started to notice that some of the kids and adults seemed to act differently towards her and her family, just because she was an Indian! *I learned about discrimination.*

Everything was going fine. During recess all I could do was to stand around and watch, because of the cumbersome cast; running or jumping was definitely out of the question. Some kids questioned why, but I couldn't answer them. They made me feel self-conscious.

Then one day at school the unthinkable happened. During recess, some of the boys had sticks and were poking me with them; laughing and joking about how round I was. I could not believe this was happening. How could people be so cruel? I just laughed it off, but their repeated antics started to create doubt in me, and eventually I refused to go back to school. I still kept my appointments at the hospital, but pretty much remained by myself. In the back of my mind I wondered what the white coats were looking for. It seemed as if they were always trying to find something else wrong with me. *This is my first bout with depression, but there is no one to talk to about my feelings.*

I was adamant about not going back to school. The white coats were suggesting to my parents that I be placed in an institution. My mother would not have this though, citing that she wanted me to live and grow up in a normal environment. While everyone was planning my future, it was time to take off the cast, and that was my only priority. This was the first time I was excited about going to the hospital. Mom helped me change into a hospital gown and a nurse assisted me in getting into a wheelchair. I'm feeling nervous, because I couldn't see my mother as the nurse wheeled me into this large, brightly lit room. There were numerous stretchers and beds in a row; some had the curtains drawn while some patients just sat and waited to be looked after. The nurse helped me onto one of the beds, and closed the curtains halfway. I felt so alone as I lay there waiting, my imagination started working overtime. *How will they get this cast off of me?*

When I saw a white coat approach the bed, I knew it was time. He barely acknowledged me as he took off my hospital gown and stood by my left side. He held what looked like a pizza slicer in his right hand and placed it at the top of the cast, between my breasts, and flicked a switch. As soon as I heard the whirring sound I panicked and immediately tensed up. *This thing could cut me in half!*

He turned off the machine and told me to just relax and breathe slowly. His words were comforting; however, I grasped both sides of the stretcher/bed, closed my eyes, grimaced and held on for dear life. When the machine stopped I opened my eyes, lifted my head and saw that the cast was cut right down the middle. I slowly moved my hands down my body and there is not a scratch on me. Then he stood at my mid section, grasped both sides of the cast and started ripping it apart. There was nothing that could compare the sound of that, but it was something I would never forget.

I'm not sure how long I lay there, but it felt so elated to be able to take deep breaths. When the white coat helped me to sit up, I slouched forward and it felt good. When he helped me stand up I felt dizzy and weak at first. That's when I noticed this young man sitting on the stretcher across from me, staring,

I suddenly realized that I was naked, except for my panties. I felt so humiliated and covered myself as I went looking for mom. She wasn't far away at all and helped me get dressed. After a short lecture from another white coat about taking it easy, like no running, jumping, etc., we went home. *I'm still an outpatient.*

I felt like a new person as we walked out of the hospital. The cast was so heavy and since I left school my hair was slowly growing back. I couldn't help feeling different and wondered how the kids in the neighborhood would treat me.

Nothing much changed. The white coats have finally made a decision to send me to a school that was specifically designed for crippled children. We went on a tour of the facility. The school had the smell and cleanliness of a hospital, and there were no white coats to be seen which was a relief. I did not have to worry about stairs either. There weren't any.

Most of the other students were in wheelchairs, or using crutches, or had missing limbs and the classrooms were big enough to accommodate the wheelchairs. I felt confused, because I could walk, run and jump. *I wondered why I am here.*

I sat in the back of the classroom. Everyday, around noon, just before class ended each student was given a half pint of milk to drink. I didn't like milk and kept telling that to the teacher, but I still had to drink one. Well right behind my desk were numerous plants and I would water them with the white drink. When they finally caught me they stopped forcing me to drink the milk. *Was anyone listening to me*?

After lunch I went for my physiotherapy. Even though one was allowed to try out any of the equipment there, I spent the majority of the time practicing to walk. The sessions would last for an hour and a half and the rest of the day was spent on social skills. I really felt comfortable here and got along well with the other students. There was no competition or judgments towards each other at all. I even got to act in two school plays, The Ugly Duckling and Thumbelina. It was fun being part of a group and working as a team.

When I got home from school things were so different. As I explained all the fun and creative things I was doing, and learned at school, it seemed that no one was really interested, except my mom. Dad and my brothers didn't really listen or care. I felt like I didn't matter.

I was the only kid in the neighborhood that got bussed to school. The bus would pick me up and then drop me off the same time as regular school hours. Some of the kids in the neighborhood mocked me because of it, and yet I was going to school just like them.

Unless dad took us for a drive, the weekends didn't change all that much. Everyone in the house usually ended up downstairs at my step grandfather's place. It was a lot of fun; many people coming and going. Some stayed and when they started walking funny and acting silly mom made us go upstairs and get ready for bed. My sleep was usually interrupted by noises of banging and people arguing; sounding loud and harsh. I got scared and pulled the blankets up over my head. Sometimes I even cried myself to sleep.

I'm 10 years old and have been going through this healing process for almost five years now. I feel confused most of the time; trying to adjust/understand an existence in different environments; hospital, home and school.

Chapter 7

I was still an outpatient and had an appointment at a hospital I had never been to. On the way there I was feeling restless to begin with and then overheard mom and dad mention Cobalt treatment. A radioactive substance used in this type of therapy. High-energy gamma rays emitted by Cobalt are directed at tumors deep within the body to destroy diseased cells.

Mom helped me undress and put on a gown. When the nurse came I was taken, alone to an area of the hospital that was really desolate. The surroundings seemed so surreal. I felt very apprehensive and was scared out of my wits. Something awful was about to happen. We stopped in front of a black cube shaped room that had windows all around. I just knew by the look of the machine hanging over a steel table that this is not a typical x-ray treatment. The table was ice cold and I shivered as the lady in the white coat helped me lay down and adjusted my body until she was satisfied. Then she left me and entered a glass booth. That's when I realized that she did not put a lead shield on me. I was so scared as I lay there not knowing what to expect. As I heard the machine revving up, this woman appeared out of nowhere. It was my nana. But she is in Heaven. Not a word was spoken between us and I felt a profound peacefulness as I closed my eyes. The sensation that rippled through my body was like nothing I had ever experienced. I knew that I had been sterilized, but never realized the ramifications of this until late into my teens and twenties. As soon as the machine stopped nana was gone and I felt so alone again.

My thoughts were focused on what I had just gone through as the white coat helped me sit up. The nurse came in, helped me into the wheelchair, and took me back to the waiting room, where mom helped me get dressed. I breathed a sigh of relief, because it meant that there was no hospital stay this time and so we went home.

During summer holidays the school sent me to a camp specifically designed for crippled children. I was nervous and scared as I got on the bus; mom could not come with me. Most of the kids were from my school, but I still felt alone. It always seemed as if I was either going away or being taken away. I harbored these feelings of separation and abandonment. The bus took us to a place called Blue Mountain in Collingwood. When we arrived I saw beautiful lake surrounded by huge mountains and lush green forests. It was a striking scene. There were cabins scattered all over the place and they were numbered. Each of us was assigned to one of the five beds contained within one of the cabins and it reminded me of the ward in the hospital. Since there was no electricity, it took a while for my eyes to adjust to the black nights. A larger cabin doubled as a dining hall and an activities room. The days were filled with all kinds of things to do; making crafts, playing games and swimming. The counselors were great as they were very helpful and supportive.

The evening campfires were a special time. We all sat around a campfire, singing songs and roasting marsh mellows. Every night before we turned in, someone would play taps on a trumpet and we would all sing, "Day is done. Gone the sun... Gone the moon..." and that's when I always became homesick.

I got into trouble once, because I wanted to explore the surroundings and talked some other kids, who could walk, to come with me. We arranged to meet at a specific spot one night after supper and just started walking into the forest. The sun had not gone down completely and when you looked up, the sun's rays sparkled like bright stars through the tops of the trees. We lost all track of time and before we knew it we were standing in a very dark forest. After climbing a little hill surrounded by bushes we just sat there wondering what to do. We were lost. I was a bit nervous, but didn't say anything. Then suddenly there is a noise coming from the nearby bushes. We all huddled together in terror, but then when we saw two tiny lights that looked like a pair of eyes coming toward us. I pointed it out to the other kids and right away I thought it was a bear. I was not the only one because we all panicked and screamed.

As these eyes came closer, we realized that they were flashlights and breathed a sigh of relieve. It was two camp counselors, looking for us. They helped us get up and took us back to camp. Not long after that incident everyone was instructed to start packing up. We were all going home.

Mom and dad met me at the bus terminal and when we got home my brothers didn't seem too be interested in hearing about all the wonderful adventures I had. *I wonder if I matter.*

When it was time to go back to school, I tried to get out of going. Mom was standing at the top of the stairs and watching me as the bus driver came into the house. When I got close to the bottom I pretended to twist my ankle, limped to the front door and crouched down on the floor. Without a word, the bus driver walked over to me, picked me up and carried me onto the bus. As soon as I got to school, one of the attendants carried me to the physiotherapy room right away. I could not get away with anything.

Chapter 8

It was 1958 and my aunt and uncle had four children by now; two girls and two boys. The oldest was 4 years old and I treated her as if she was my little sister. My youngest brother was five now and my other two brothers who were seven and nine, were usually outside playing. I didn't feel comfortable hanging out with the kids in the neighborhood, and usually stayed in the house. We lived a block away from Alan Gardens; a huge park that was as large as a whole city block. On Saturdays, if dad were working, all of us, including my aunt and her kids, would usually go there. They had a huge playground and a greenhouse, where we spent most of the afternoon just having fun.

I'm not sure how I ended up in the park one Sunday morning, but it was quite an experience. Lots of grown ups were there and not too many kids. Throughout the park there were at least ten or more people crowded in a circle listening to someone. I was curious and walked over and stuck my head in between some people to see what was going on. There was a man standing on a box discussing God "about sinning and going to hell if you don't believe in him." I listened, of course, trying to understand the conversation and sometimes the man's voice would get very loud and angry. *Who is this God?*

During supper I told dad about the park thing, and he couldn't give me a straight answer, except to say, "When you're dead your dead, and six feet in the ground." His reaction surprised me and there was no reasoning with him at all. So I put it in the back of my mind. Until one day, while I was playing outside I heard dad shouting something about leaving the kids alone. I went to see what was going on and he was standing on the veranda, yelling at some people; ranting and raving about brainwashing them with this god nonsense and to get out of here. He sounded very angry. Of course, I was filled with curiosity and decided to investigate what God was all about. There were a lot of churches in the neighborhood and I picked the closest one to home. I wasn't scared at all just a bit guilty, because I was going behind dads back.

As I approached this church I saw a group of people entering and sneaked in behind them. It was a peaceful place and the strong aroma of wood was everywhere. As I looked ahead of me, I could see rows and rows of benches and a lot of people mingling about to find a seat. I jumped as someone tapped me on the shoulder and said that I belonged upstairs with the other children, in Sunday school.

I slowly made my way up the stairs and could hear a woman's voice. When I found the room it reminded me of school. This young girl, who was the teacher, asked me my name, introduced me to everyone, handed me a Bible, and told me to take a seat. There are at least ten other children in the room and most of them were younger than me. As I settled into one of the wooden chairs, she continued where she had left off, discussing the difference between right and wrong; if you are good and obeyed God you would go to heaven, emphasizing how wonderful and peaceful a place it is. If you do bad things you would go to hell, which she emphasized as being a horrible and frightening place. I felt confused; was God punishing me? Did I do something bad? My whole being reflected on the accident, the hospital and being treated differently, and kept my adventure in Church a secret.

It was difficult to discuss religion at home. Whenever I brought it up dad would become really upset and chant 'when your dead, you're dead. You're six feet under and that's that!' As I got older I investigated different churches and religions, but never took it seriously.

In June I turned eleven and summer holidays would soon be here. The day started out as usual, we had finished breakfast and were in the front room (mom and dad's room) watching television. Dad had just left for work, when suddenly we smelled smoke. Mom told us to stay where we were while she went to investigate. She came back into the room carrying my youngest brother, and when she put him down, she ran to the window. I squeezed in front of her and saw dad walking down the street. Her voice sounded a bit frantic as she called him. When he turned around she kept screaming, "FIRE! FIRE!". He ran into the house and I could hear him yelling, "FIRE!" As he came upstairs the smoke was getting thicker and thicker. It was scary, because in order for us to get out we had to pass my brothers' bedroom where the fire started. My youngest brother was playing with matches in the bedroom closet. We covered our faces and quickly ran down the stairs and out into the street. My aunt and uncle, and their four children had no other escape but the roof.

It was complete and utter chaos. Everything happened so quickly. They were rescued and the fire was put out. No one was hurt. Unfortunately, the damage was so extensive that no one could live on the third floor. My aunt and uncle moved to the west end of Toronto. They seemed so far away now. I missed my cousins a lot and when we would go and visit them, I would sometimes sleep over.

Everything had to be replaced; floors, doors, etc. Dad was still learning about the painting business, which helped a lot. My uncles pitched in and also helped. While repairs were going on my brothers had to sleep in the front room with mom and dad. As I said earlier my room was at the end of the hall so I was away from a lot of goings on. I always felt left out. Once all the repairs had been done, the house looked better than it did before the fire. Dad had done a great job. My aunt and uncle eventually moved back to the third floor and I was happy for them at that time.

As I got older, I often wondered why they moved back to the third floor; it seemed to me that they had a lot more room at the other house. My grandfather always seemed in control; especially regarding money and booze. He probably bribed them. I noticed too that Dad and my step grandfather's relationship always seemed a little tense and this fire made things even worse.

Another year has passed and my aunt and uncle had another baby boy, which made five cousins now. Roller skates were the rage now and a lot of kids in the neighborhood had them. I was no different and begged mom for a pair. She got them, but I was only allowed to use one skate. That was good enough for me. So here I was. I had one skate on and I was barreling down the street. Somehow I tripped and hit my head on the corner step of the house next door to us. I was very calm as the blood began dripping down my face and walked in to the house to call mom. As soon as she saw me she panicked, called a taxi and we headed for the hospital.

She coached me all the way there into not telling the doctor I was roller-skating. I felt that I had done something bad and started to get scared. *If I told the white coat the truth what would they do to me?*

I felt nervous as the white coat who examined me and I was almost in hysterics as I told him that I tripped and fell, which really was the truth. I got ten stitches on my forehead and we went home. I felt confused.

I didn’t miss any school and could go out and play after dinner too. Dad would get upset with me regarding these medical issues. I knew that times were still tough too; money was scarce. Sometimes when he got drunk, he would complain that every time I went to the hospital it cost him money. His ruminating made me feel like a burden on the family. *His drinking scares me.*

I ended up taking out the stitches in my forehead myself so I wouldn’t have to go to the hospital and make dad pay for it.

Friday and Saturday nights seemed to be party time for the adults. My brothers and I had fun too. Watching people stagger around and talk funny. Sometimes mom and dad would go out, and my uncle would watch us. Sunday mornings were quiet. I was in the bathroom and heard my other uncle yelling at my mother. He was calling her name. He was yelling something about the baby. I ran to the landing and stood at the top of the stairs. My uncle had just reached the bottom as mom came out of her room. I could not believe what I saw. At first I thought he was carrying a rag doll and then I realized that it was my cousin. He was not moving and my uncle was crying. This is the first time I ever saw a man cry and I really didn’t understand what was going on. I knew that something awful had just happened.

Anna Pinack Carrabs

Everything in the house changed that day and I didn't understand why. When we weren't in school mom and dad kept us busy so I don't recall too much, except the day I heard heavy footsteps coming up the stairs. I ran to the landing and saw some men in black suits go up to the third floor. They weren't up there long and when they came back down, my uncle was with them with his hands behind his back. I never saw him again for a long time. He went to prison for two years. All my cousins were taken away and put into foster homes. Now my aunt was truly alone.

It was 1961 and there was a lot of tension in the house. It felt so empty. I couldn't understand what had happened, and there was no one to talk to about how I felt. I missed my cousins a lot.

Nothing was the same anymore, except for school. I was playing outside and came in to ask mom something. I could see her and my aunt in my grandfather's kitchen. They were arguing about something, and didn't know that I was there. I tried to interrupt and couldn't so I begin tugging on my mother's skirt. All of a sudden my aunt turns around and slaps me in the face. Mom immediately turns around and slapped her back.

They started fighting, hitting and shoving each other. Mom was pushing her sister out onto the back porch and that's when I lost it. I got scared and screamed for them to stop it! "Stop it! Stop it!" I screamed until everything went blank. *What have I done? This was my fault. From that moment on I was hesitant to ask anyone for anything.*

Chapter 9

One Saturday morning, after breakfast dad told us that we were going for a drive. As he drove along Gerrard Street he informed us that we were going to see our new house. My brothers and I looked at each other speechless. Wow, so many things went through my mind as he turned north on Pape Avenue. There was a big industrial plant on your right and railway tracks straight ahead. After driving over the tracks, to the left was another big industrial unit. Just north of that was a row of six houses. Ours was the fifth house. I could not believe it, two stories with a big veranda and a lawn. There were six steps that led up to the veranda, and it was the width of the house. As you came in the front door there was a vestibule and a second door. The hallway was about four feet long with stairs leading to the second floor. To your right was a glass door that led into the living room. There was a sliding partition that separated the living room from the dining room, which was eventually taken down and it became one big room. The floors were all hard wood, except for the kitchen, and it was as big as my Uncle Joe's.

There was a door to your left, which led to the basement. The stairs were creaky and small, which made me nervous. The cellar was one big room and the light wasn't very bright, which made it look spooky, especially in the corners. The floor was made out of concrete and the walls, concrete blocks. This reminded me of the hospital basement and the not so happy memories. When you turned left at the foot of the stairs there was what looked like a big black oven. To the right and farther into the room, there was a wooden partition, with an arch for a doorway. My brothers and I saw a mountain of black coal in one corner. This was shoveled into the big black oven that heated the house.

Back on the main floor and into the kitchen was a door that led to the back of the house. There was a small porch and a good-sized backyard. The grass was patchy and at the end of the yard stood a small garage that led to a laneway.

We went back into the house and to the second floor. At the top of the stairs was a bedroom or back room. This was to be my room. The window looked out onto the backyard and I could see a school nearby. To the right of my room was the bathroom and next to that was another bedroom. This was my brothers' room. Their window faced the side of the house, from which you could also see some of the backyard. At the end of the hall was a third room, which was the width of the house. This was mom and dad's room and their windows faced Pape Avenue.

I'm not sure how my brothers felt, but I had mixed feelings. I was excited about all the room we had compared to where we lived now, but deep down inside I was scared and confused and focused on the neighbors. Even though it was probably better, I carry with me emotional baggage.

It was 1961 and winter, when we move into our new home. I was excited, because mom was going to have another baby. There was so much to be done, with dad working most of the time now, and my brothers and I doing what we could. We needed help. My uncle David came over and helped out a lot. In the evening he and my dad would get drunk and sometimes he would sleep on the couch in the front room. Their actions reminded me of our old neighborhood.

When the time came to go back to school I found out, without any explanation, that I had been enrolled back into the public school system, which I had been away from for a little over two years. I would be going into grade six too, and I was scared. This was going to be a real adjustment and I worried about the kids; how would they treat me?

The previous school I had attended seemed to be geared toward rehabilitation and not education, so I didn't take it seriously, and I didn't have a clue that I was being graded. It appeared to be more about having fun than learning.

Mom came with me the first day. I was so scared, but she reassured me that everything would be all right and after registering at the office, mom helped me find my classroom. As I knocked on the door, she left. *I feel abandoned.*

The teacher introduced me to the rest of the class. I heard some of the students snicker, and immediately flashed back to that one day in school, during recess, when some of the boys had sticks and they were poking at me and making fun of my size. There was nothing I could do but shrug it off, find an empty desk and try to do my best, but I couldn't help that feeling that I was different. The transition back to public school was difficult to say the least.

My brothers didn't seem to have a problem adjusting at all and made friends easily. The schoolyard was the place to hang out. My oldest brother would always be found there with some of his friends. I tried to hang out with them, he would start pushing and shoving me around. Just picking on me for no reason at all. Other times, when my oldest brother's friends weren't around, he was fine. I took advantage of these times, and had fun with him.

I was having difficulty comprehending most of the subjects and felt distracted by some of the other students. Mom was very supportive and always encouraged me to do my best. Dad was the opposite; always finding fault with me. When I complained to mom, she made excuses for his behavior, saying that he was just kidding. *His drinking scares me.*

In March my new baby brother arrived and it was awesome. Not only that, but just before my fourteenth birthday, the white coats gave me a clean bill of health and informed my parents that I would probably live a relatively healthy life. This was great news to me; thinking I would never have to see a white coat again. Because of my previous medical issues; being segregated, it was an opportunity to bond with my new baby brother, which never happened with any of my other brothers.

My baby brother was such a delight and a distraction from issues at home. I spent as much time as possible with him. I didn't like it when he got sick and felt so sad for him. When I played with him and he got hurt dad would chastise me, and make me feel so bad. He would be drunk, of course, and ruminate about me being sick and how much money I had cost him. It made me feel like I was a burden on the family. There was no one to confide in. *Sometimes I would wet the bed.*

My birthday was coming and I was quite excited, because the school year was almost over. It had been quite a challenge trying to keep up and fit in, but it paid off. I passed into Grade seven. I was so proud of myself. Apparently I had just enough credits.

During summer holidays the schoolyard was the place to hang out and if dad weren't working we would go for a drive, if not in the country, then to the old neighborhood. I started to notice the difference between neighborhoods; ours was so much cleaner and brighter. Our neighbors were nice and not creepy. My aunt had a baby girl, which changed the atmosphere of the house a little. Her other children are still in foster care and I missed them a lot. I would get to hang out with the girls across the street including my Indian friend. I enjoyed these times away from home.

Chapter 10

The summer seemed to go by so fast and I start thinking about school again. Mom came with me the first day. It was located at Broadview and Dundas and taught only grades, seven and eight. For half the day you would rotate every forty-five minutes to a different class or subject and the other half the day would be spent in your homeroom. I did have problems with some of my subjects. The biggest challenge of all was the stairs. When it was time to change classes the other students would run up and down the stairs. It made me so nervous that I was afraid I would be pushed and fall, so I took my time holding onto the banister. I got some funny stares from some of the students, and began to feel self-conscious. Whenever I complained about something that bothered me, I had the feeling of not being heard at all, just criticized and manipulated. Dad's comeback would be that I didn't know what I was talking about. *I am so frustrated and probably came across as being angry.*

It was 1962 and I had adjusted well living in this neighborhood. School was hard and I didn't get any help at home. I found grade seven very difficult, because I just couldn't seem to comprehend most of my subjects. I was easily distracted by the other students too and found myself getting into trouble. The teachers were not really attentive to my needs, and I did have problems asking for help. All I could do was to make the best of it. *I think walking to and from school is therapy. I liked being alone to gather my thoughts.*

My uncle Kevin came home. Their little girl was a year and a half now, but their other children were still in foster care. Shortly after he got settled in, arrangements were made for them to have supervised visits with their children at our house. It was a bit awkward, but it was nice to see them all together again. These visits turned out to be good, and they were continued, but I can't remember for how long.

My birthday was coming, which meant, summer holidays were coming and I was excited. Just after my birthday mom informed me that I had a doctor's appointment. I was feeling a bit nervous because my back hadn't been bothering me too much. We didn't have a family doctor so we had to go to the hospital.

When we arrived, we were instructed to go to Door five. It was a small room with a bed and chair. I was instructed to take all my clothes off, including underwear and to roll down my socks to my ankles, put on a hospital gown and have a seat in the waiting room. *I'm feeling really anxious.*

The waiting room was full of older men and women, with their socks rolled down to their ankles too. The atmosphere is just dreadful and my throat was getting dry. *Something awful is going to happen.*

When my name is called, we followed the nurse who took us into an examination room. There were two other nurses and a white coat in the room. The stretcher bed looked normal with a pillow for your head, but at the other end there were these strange metal cups on each side. I was instructed to lie on the bed and put my feet in the metal cups.

I don't remember the white coat introducing herself to us, and without any warning she took off the hospital gown and covered me with a sheet. I was speechless as she headed to the end of the bed where my feet were. She spread my legs and proceeded to examine my genitals; prodding and probing me. I closed my eyes and gripped the side of the bed feeling violated, humiliated and helpless.

When it is all over she covered me up, pat me on the forehead and made a comment about my behavior. I was very quiet, withdrawn and not a happy child. Then she proceeded to take my mother aside and converse with her for some time. *I feel ashamed, angry and betrayed.*

Mom never explained a thing to me, and my confidence in her diminished. As we headed back to the cubicle and changed into my street clothes I felt relieved, because it meant that I could go home. On our way there I wondered what else was wrong with me? *This is my first of many internal examinations, because I am not menstruating yet.*

I felt so frustrated at times, not only with medical issues, but school too. There wasn't a lot of support at home, mostly criticism and no one to talk too. The school year was almost over, which was great and with hard work and determination I manage to pass into Grade eight. Again, I had just enough credits and was really proud of myself.

During the summer holiday's, I enjoyed visiting the old neighborhood. Sometimes I was allowed to go there on my own and spend time with my step grandfather, aunt and uncles. I enjoyed these visits because I was not judged by any of them. When it was time to go home I felt terrible again because I never knew what to expect.

On the weekends, if dad weren't working we would take drives out to his uncle's farm or to the beach. If we didn't go anywhere, we'd get together and play cards in the kitchen. It was fun, until the criticism got to be too much. I got very unsure of myself and full of doubt. Dad would be drinking, of course, which made me nervous. *He usually picks on me.*

I enjoyed challenging myself and sometimes I'd go into the schoolyard and play tennis against the wall. If my older brother was there I'd try to hang out with him, but he was so mean sometimes and pushed me away. Of course, his friends were witness to this behavior too and they'd think it was funny.

The summer holidays always seemed to go by so fast. When it was time to go back to school, I felt a bit anxious. I knew it was the same school, but the adjustment, at first, was hard, for I never knew what to expect from the other students. Homeroom was very easygoing this time. There were no boys in the class, and the room housed fewer students than the year earlier. There were a number of subjects that I really liked this time.

Home Economics was very interesting and lots of fun. I learned how to sew, cook, and do arts and crafts. Some of the projects in class took teamwork and I enjoyed that because I felt connected. Mom had a sewing machine, so we worked on some of the sewing projects together. I would cut out a pattern for pants, and she would instruct me as I put it all together. She had a lot of patience and was really creative herself, which she probably learned from her mother, my nana.

I liked English Literature. Speech and Drama were my favorites. I was learning how to do stage lighting and make up and doing some drawing and painting. I enjoyed the aspect of the lessons.

During a school play I had a chance to put into practice what I had learned. I did the stage lighting and applied make up to some of the students who were acting on stage. Everything turned out just great and I was filled with such enthusiasm. I was so excited when I got home, but to my family, it didn't appear to matter what I am doing. There just didn't seem to be any enthusiasm or direction. I found myself gravitating towards some girls in my class who made fun of a few teachers and disrupted the class. It was fun sometimes and I figured that if I went along with them they wouldn't pick on me. *These girls treat me like I mattered to them.*

One morning at school, before the first bell, I went into the washroom. Half of my class was in there smoking cigarettes. I was handed one and thought well, mom and dad smoked so I figured it would be all right. We were just standing around smoking and chatting when suddenly one of the teachers happened to walk in. I was really scared. Half of the students in my class, including myself got a detention. *This is my first detention of many.*

When I got home, I explained to mom what happened and it was only because I was there, and not because I was smoking. I must admit that I felt guilty for lying to her.

Not long after that incident at school mom made me stay home to help her clean the house while my brothers went out to play. This didn't seem fair at all, especially when she cleaned their room, but not mine.

My youngest brother was two years old by now. There was a community center on the corner of Pape and Gerrard and a park right next to it. We spend a lot of time there and had a great time. When he got hurt, dad always yelled at me and made me feel stupid; then he brought up the past about how much money my medical bills kept costing him. His comments always made me feel like I was a burden to the family. *His drinking scares me.*

Chapter 11

My sixteenth birthday soon arrived and at school I started to hear rumors that our class was for students with learning difficulties. Some students chided that we were dummies and their comments really upset me. *I'm not stupid. I got sick and missed a lot of school because of medical issues.*

My impression was that special education was only for troublemakers. No one had ever tried to help me, and at home there was definitely a lack of communication and interest. Some of the girls in class were so mischievous, and I was very naïve. I knew that I was getting into trouble, but I felt like I belonged. I started to develop a lackadaisical attitude toward my education.

The school year was almost over and everyone was getting excited about graduation. I wasn't. One day during class, I was told to go to the Principal's office. I was so nervous, wondering what I did wrong now. He told me to have a seat and proceeded to tell me that I would be graduating in June. Oh my God! I was in shock as he went on to explain that I had won the Jesse Ketchum Award for Punctuality. The award was a choice of two different books, which would be handed out on the evening of the Graduation. I chose the book, "All About Art".

As I made my way back to class, my mind was racing and I felt weak in the knees. Nothing like this had ever happened to me. I never felt worthy of anything. As I entered the classroom everyone's eyes were upon me as I sat down at my desk. The girl who sat next to me on my right, asked me what had happened. As soon as I tried to explain I started crying hysterically and had to leave the classroom.

When I got home from school I put on a serious look as I told mom that I was called down to the principal's office. She looked mad at first, but when I told her what happened (I left out the crying part) her expression changed and she told me that she was so proud of me. *I'm nervous just thinking about getting up on stage in front of the whole school to accept my award. I really don't like a lot of attention focused on me and very seldom admitted my feelings, because I figured no one would understand.*

Money was scarce and it was difficult finding something for me to wear. I was a big girl and kind of relieved, because I might not be able to go. Then mom decided to let me wear one of her suits, so now I had no choice. I was very preoccupied about this graduation thing, because I had to get up on stage in front of the whole school. I didn't think of anything else, but that.

On the day of my birthday, nobody made a fuss. In the early afternoon mom sent me down to my aunts to pick something up for her, and told me to take my time. When I got back home and walked into the dining room everyone yelled happy birthday. Boy, did I jump! A surprise Party! A lot of kids were there and everything felt perfect. Everything was just great; until we played spin the bottle and a boy kissed me. I got up, ran into the kitchen and out the back door.

Mom and dad were right behind me and I was hysterical. The only affection I ever received or felt was from the nurses at the hospital. This incident was too emotional for me; I panicked and ran away. When I finally calmed down everyone had gone home and the party was over. No one in the family said anything about the party and yet I felt as if I had done something wrong. I had no one to confide in. Everyone must have thought that I was a mental case. *What is wrong with me?*

I couldn't help, but feel like I had done something terrible. Not long after the incident I was in my room, sitting on my bed and contemplating life; the school year was almost over. I'd be graduating and wondering about grade nine, especially what the students would be like. *Everything seems to be moving too fast.*

Just then dad stood in the doorway. I jumped and felt uneasy, but before I could say anything he proceeded to tell me that, "I really

didn't matter much to him, that his sons meant more to him, because they would carry on his name," and he just walked away.
Oh my God, I could not believe what I had just heard. This man, my father, did not like me. The feeling of rejection was overwhelming. I never told anyone about this incident and put on a front, acting like nothing happened between us. *What is wrong with me!*

This incident affected my relationship with men and I had to come to terms with the fact that perhaps this was why my brothers' attitude towards me was disrespectful at times, especially my oldest brother. My self-esteem plummeted and I felt very insignificant and meaningless. *I want to leave home.*

At school, everyone was looking forward to graduation day, but me. I just couldn't forget what dad had said to me. This was my fault, and I didn't like myself very much. During one of my classes I overheard one of the girls talking about getting a job after school at a downtown hospital. I told her I was interested, and before the school year was over, we went together and applied for the job. We were both hired. We started when school was finished. I knew mom was happy for me.

Graduation day had finally arrived and I was very nervous. The auditorium was filling up and as mom and I found our seats. My attention was focused on the stage, because sooner or later I would have to go up there. The principal made a few speeches regarding the school year and praised the graduates. Then it was time for the awards to be handed out. When I heard my name being called I got up and carefully walked toward the stairs leading up onto the stage. I was practically holding my breath and being very extremely cautious not to trip. I managed to trip on the second step going up, but quickly caught my balance. With a red flushed face and shaky hands I accepted my award, said "Thank you" and quickly returned back to my seat.

After all the awards were handed out the principal informed everyone that the dance was being held in the gymnasium in an hour or so. We went outside for some fresh air and mom took some pictures, but I decided not to go to the dance. We started for home and on the way there I thought a lot about my future. I thought about my new job and about leaving home.

Two days after graduation I met up with my schoolmate and we went to work. I was excited and eager but didn't want to show it. We were working in the kitchen with five other girls. Each of us had a specific duty to perform and work as a team getting the patients' meals ready and delivering them on time. It felt good to belong, especially when I knew what was expected of me. My first day went well, no criticisms. On my days off I enjoyed spending time with my youngest brother. If I worked weekends I missed out on a lot of family outings, and yet in the back of my mind I wondered if they missed me at all. *I feel so alone at times.*

I got paid approximately $50.00 every two weeks and felt so independent. It was great having money. I would give mom $15.00, and she never complained about it, but not dad, no way. He didn't think it was enough. He would start to talk about my previous medical needs and how much money it had cost him. When I complained to mom about this, she told me that he was only joking. *I feel guilty; like a burden on the family.*

I worked in the kitchen with other girls and our job was to get the meals ready and deliver them to patients in the hospital. The trays would come down the conveyor belt with the patients' menus, which they would fill out the previous day. When the tray was complete and ready to go, we would stack them on a trolley. We worked in pairs when it was time to deliver them.

The summer went by fast and was almost over. I had to go and register at this new school, before starting grade nine. I was nervous and didn't know what to expect, as mom and I approached the school. It was huge and reminded me of an old castle. When mom and I got there, the halls were full of teachers and students wandering around, very chaotic. The school's curriculum was commercial, all business. When we finally found the office, finished registering and got my timetable, we took a tour and located my homeroom. On the way back home I thought about the other students. The classroom was much bigger, including the blackboard. There were at least 30 desks, which meant more students. Homeroom was on the ground floor and I liked the idea of rotating to different classes throughout the day.

The next day at work, my boss called me into her office. I was wondering what I did wrong. She asked me, "If I would like to continue working when I go back to school." Well, I was beside myself. I must have done a good job and said, "Yes." On the way home I was excited, but in the back of my mind I wondered if I could handle both.

Chapter 12

My first day at school went well. All the students in my class were girls and it reminded me of grade eight. The stairs were still a real issue for me. Sometimes I would be late getting to my next class, and the teacher would give me attitude. *Nobody bothers to ask me why or understands what I'm going through.*

Halfway through the school year it was suggested that I needed glasses. Apparently I wasn't paying enough attention in class. There was no OHIP in place and we didn't have a family doctor so I had to go to the hospital. *It's going to cost dad money.*

When mom and I got there a nurse put me in a wheelchair and we went to the basement. I was feeling edgy and worried, because I could walk. The nurse left mom sitting in the hall as we entered an examination room. There was one white coat in there that told me to stay seated in the wheelchair. He did a lot of different examinations on my eyes, and there was nothing said, which made me feel uncomfortable to say the least. When he completed the examination he told me that I needed glasses, adding that I probably sat in the back of the classroom, which made it difficult to see the blackboard in the first place. So my attention was not focused on anything and that was why I was fat. I couldn't believe what I just heard. Dad's attitude towards me comes to mind. *What is wrong with me?*

He wheeled me out into the hall and called the nurse. He gave mom the prescription for my glasses and explained to her that he will be sending a report to my school recommending that I sit closer to the front of the class. I didn't say anything to mom about the white coat's comment, as we made our way home. It sure was upsetting to me and played on my mind. *I've always felt self-conscious about my body, and now I have to wear glasses.*

At first I only wore the glasses when I got to school and of course at home. I was sitting in front of the class now trying to look busy, hoping that the teacher didn't pick on me to answer questions. If I got it wrong the other students might think I was stupid and would laugh at me.

I started hanging around with some of the girls in my class who were disruptive and picked on other students and teachers. I didn't take my education seriously and started acting out with them. I figured that if I were to be friends with them they wouldn't pick on me. I paid the consequences by getting detentions, which interfered with my work schedule sometimes. The catalyst here was that these girls liked me and it felt good. *I wasn't getting a lot of help or attention at home, or in school.*

Gym and swimming was another class I dreaded, because some of the girls would laugh and make comments about my body; saying that I was top heavy. In the locker room I would overhear some of them talking and complaining about cramps when they got their periods. *I know that I'm a big girl!*

When I got home I asked mom about this. She looked embarrassed and would change the subject, and didn't pursue it. In the back of my mind it was a mystery. I'm sixteen years old and wonder why I haven't experienced it yet.

That same night I woke up with terrible cramps and there was blood in my underwear. I was in a panic when I called mom. She didn't say much as she handed me what she uses, without any explanation and that was it. It was an uncomfortable experience to say the least. *What's the big secret?*

This was my first and only period, which only lasted three days. Of course, the white coats got involved and I had many internal examinations. It was humiliating and I wondered what else was wrong with me. I couldn't help but think about the Cobalt treatment I had and the after effects of it.

I really enjoyed my job, but there were times when I felt such compassion for the patients, because of my own experiences doing time in the hospital. I knew how lonely it could get. I didn't think my boss liked this, because sometimes I was put in charge of the dishwasher. The dishes were placed on a conveyor belt and fed through a jet stream system. The water was very hot so when the dishes came out from the other end and hit the air they were dry and all I had to do was to stack them on the shelves. During this one shift, while I was stacking the dessert dishes to place on the shelf, they tipped over. I cut my left wrist and it wouldn't stop bleeding. One of my coworkers took me down to emergency, and left me there. I was fine until I was alone with the white coat. He asked me what happened. As I started to explain I lost control and starting crying uncontrollably. I must have been given something to calm me down, because the next thing I remembered was being home with my left wrist all bandaged up. I was off work for a few days, but couldn't get out of going to school. *I'm right handed, which is a bummer.*

School was not easy. Some of the subjects were really hard to comprehend and I was becoming more and more frustrated. No one was willing to help me with my homework. When I returned to work, it was worse. I would get home around nine o'clock in the evening, and have to do my homework. It was late and I was very tired. There was no one around to ask for help. I felt so angry and insignificant some times. The comments dad made to me kept coming to mind and I would think about leaving home. Where would I go? What would I do? I think about the goals I had set for myself and struggled to stay in school.

I was scheduled to work that coming Saturday, but I really didn't feel like going. Dad offered to drive me, which I thought was unusual. I didn't trust him, something was up, and when I approached the car there was mom in the front seat and my brothers in the back. When we got to the hospital they told me to have a good day and just drove off. *I feel as if they are abandoning me and that I do not matter.*

During my shift, all I could think about was where and what my family was up to and did they miss me. I would get teary eyed and felt like crying, and headed for the stairwell to try and calm myself down. This happened at least three or four times until my coworker followed me and asked if I was okay. I started crying hysterically and could not stop.

The next thing I remember was that I was sitting in my supervisor's office. I must have been given something, because felt very relaxed, but confused. She asked me what happened and I couldn't explain it. Trying to make sense of it myself, when Barry walked in the office to take me home.

We sat together in the streetcar, but hardly spoke at all, which made me feel guilty. We were walking up the street and almost home when he told me, that he didn't like me. Dad's attitude towards me came to mind, and now my brother. *What is wrong with me?*

I stayed home more now and felt really uncomfortable, as if I had done something terrible, but no one would say anything. I felt confused about what to do with my job for there was no one to talk to. When I thought about going back to work I felt embarrassed and decided to quit, and concentrate on my education. Besides sewing, mom was teaching me how to knit. If I made a mistake, she would make me take it all apart and start over, which was frustrating, but I never gave up. *She had so much patience and instilled in me a quality, that whenever you do anything, do it right the first time.*

We had a great time together until dad got home. I felt really tense, and defensive, but tried not to show it. Our conversations always ended up in arguments and I went to my room. Mom was always keeping the peace, and told me that dad was only joking. *What is wrong with me?*

I really wanted to leave home, but realized that my future depended on having a job. There were three subjects that I really liked, and got good grades. They were typing, business machines and English literature. So I tolerated my other subjects and persevered.

It was 1964 and near the end of grade nine when I met some girls at school who lived in my neighborhood. We started walking to school together and I hung around with one of them in particular. Her name was Stella and she was Macedonian. She had three younger sisters. We got along really well.

I was going into grade ten in September and in the back of my mind I couldn't believe it. I tried to keep busy during the summer holidays; hanging out with Stella and visiting the old neighborhood. Dad still drove us out to the country to visit with his aunt and uncle on the farm. These family outings were important, because it allowed me to bond with my family, and as long as dad didn't drink, things went relatively well. *At home I avoid dad as much as possible by staying in my room.*

The summer always seemed to go by so fast, when it was time to go back to school. It was the same old routine as grade nine, but homeroom was different; there were boys in my class, and I found it a little unsettling. Because of dad's attitude and comments towards me, I felt uptight and a little defensive around boys. *I persevere and use humor to cover up how I feel.*

Grade ten subjects were more complicated than ever. I just didn't get it! I persevered and concentrated on the subjects that I did well in. Of course, the stairs were still an issue with me. I was scared I was going to get pushed and fall down, so I usually would be late for my classes. Some of my teachers acted indifferent towards me, because of my tardiness. *But no one bothers to ask why. Nothing changes.*

There was only two months of school left and math was one of my worst subjects. We were learning about negatives and positives and I really felt frustrated. I just didn't get it and noticed that the teacher was focusing on me too much. I tried to look busy, but when the teacher asked me a question I didn't know the answer to, I felt humiliated, and just sat there, ignoring her. *I've never done anything like this before.*

On the way home from school I felt just awful. What was I doing there? I felt like I was wasting my time, and made a decision not to go back to school. I felt such a sense of relief just thinking about quitting. I was desperate as I told mom about how I felt and hoped she would understand. A couple of days later, my oldest brother went to my school and told them I wasn't coming back. I feel so relieved that I don't have to go back there. *I'm sure mom has something to do with it.*

At the dinner table nobody said a word about my decision and I couldn't help feeling guilty, like I've done something wrong. *I'm not a failure!*

I started staying away from home as much as possible, but that wasn't easy, because I had no money. Mom would help me out, but dad kept her on a strict allowance.

Some Friday nights I would go to school dances with Stella and some of the other girls. When boys were involved I felt uncomfortable and unsure of myself, but it was better than staying home. Other times I'd go to my old neighborhood and visit my aunt and uncle. My aunt and I got along really well, because she was not judgmental towards me. *Dad would always make nasty comments about her.*

They had two girls; the oldest was three and the other one and a half. It was fun playing with them. Her other children were still in foster care.

I visited the old neighborhood and would hook up with the girls who lived across the street and Cheyenne too. If we didn't stay in the neighborhood we'd hang out downtown and take in a movie. Mom would give me money to go out, but told me not to tell dad. Occasionally I would stay overnight at Cheyenne's house. Her mother, like my dad was a drinker, so we had something in common.

It was 1965; I was eighteen and really felt frustrated. I was sitting on my bed feeling really down and depressed. I got to do something with my life, and finding a job would be a priority, but I didn't know what to do and needed help. *I don't feel too confident about myself.*

Suddenly mom walked in and started to berate me about wasting my life away and that I'd better start thinking about finding a job. She walked out just as abruptly and left me with my thoughts. First dad and now mom, but I knew that she was right. I've got to do something with my life, but I was scared. When I got up enough nerve I went downstairs and admitted to her that I didn't know where or what to do, and needed help.

She helped me look through the want ads. There was a bank downtown looking for help, but there were no details about the job. I planned to go down there the next day and check it out. I didn't sleep well, but got up early, and headed out. Mom wished me luck.

When I got there the Help Wanted sign was on the front door. I went inside and asked someone about the job, was handed an application, and after the interview I felt pretty good. While, I was waiting for an answer, a woman came into the room and introduced herself as the company nurse. She asked me about my health and I told her that I did have back problems and was born with a bone disease. She excused herself and left the room. I couldn't help feeling that I had said something wrong, because the atmosphere changed. A few minutes later the person who interviewed me came into the room and told me that all the positions had been taken. I felt just dreadful as I left the building, found a phone booth, and called home. I told mom what happened. When I got home mom told me not to say anything about my past health problems. I felt really confused at this point and treated it like a secret but subconsciously I felt ashamed of myself. *What is wrong with me?*

I finally came to terms with the fact that that's what I'd have to do in order to get and keep a job. So that's what I did. I lied! The next few interviews I went on were difficult because of testing, and I didn't do well at all, but I was determined. I applied at a government office downtown and the interview went well. I had to take a typing test. I was nervous and I failed. This was one of my favorite subjects in school. They gave me another chance and this time I passed. Oh my God, I have a full time job.

I knew that I wasn't so smart, because of the lack of education I had, but I managed with courage to take a chance. The motivation was the environment I was living in; negative. My very first full time job was perfectly suited to what I was good at and that was typing. I was still leery of people, and apprehensive about my coworkers.

Throughout my working life I kept my medical issues a secret for fear of jeopardizing my employment.

I was working in a typing pool with twenty other women, young and old. It was a good time in my life, because I knew what was expected of me. After a few months, my supervisor praised me for doing a good job, and took a real liking to me. A few of my coworkers notice this, and were suggesting that I was sucking up to her. I felt centered out by their comments as if I was doing something wrong, and used my sense of humor to cover up the doubt in my mind. *Why are some people so mean?*

Chapter 13

It was 1967, and I would be twenty soon. My grandfather sold his house on Mutual Street and bought another house just down the street from us at Pape and Dundas. Of course, everyone that lived with him in the house came with him. Not long after the move my aunt and uncle were reunited with their five other children. There were seven children in that house now. I was happy for them, but it must have been a very confusing time for all of them. I know what it was like to be separated from family; the bond would never be the same.

Shortly after the move I noticed that there was more drinking and partying going on than usual. Most of the time it was at my step grandfathers house. It reminded me of the old neighborhood. I started drinking too and nobody stopped me. It made me feel calm and relaxed. Life wasn't so bad after all. No one knew that I had started to smoke and the schoolyard was convenient for that. One Saturday morning I was sitting on the schoolyard steps having a cigarette and contemplating my life. My job was going well and it was great having my own money. What upset me was every payday I would give mom some money. Of course, dad would protest saying that it wasn't enough. Why was he always criticizing me? Sometimes I noticed that my other brothers were doing the same thing. *Are all men like this?*

All of a sudden I heard a car coming and threw away my cigarette, but it was too late. It was dad and he started shouting at me that he's going to tell mom that I was smoking. I couldn't believe what just happened. Why was he always out to get me? *What is wrong with me?*

Well, I knew I had to go home sooner or later. Mom was waiting for me and I expected a lecture, but she just said that as long as I could buy my own cigarettes it was fine with her. What a relief. *I think about leaving home.*

At home nothing much changed, so most of my weekends were spent visiting the old neighborhood. When I hooked up with Cheyenne, we sometimes went downtown and hung out. At that time I was introduced to this young man, who was a bit older than me and I liked him.

He picked me up one night and we drove down to Cherry Beach. I was very nervous, because I had never been alone with a boy, and wasn't sure what to expect. We talked for a while and then he kissed me. I felt absolutely paralyzed and succumbed to his will. It felt so good to be held and touched that I lost all control of all my senses. He must have really liked me. My emotional needs were being met and I felt needed. When I got home I just went up to my room, and thought about what had happened.

Stella and I started talking a lot about moving out too. I felt thrilled about the idea. My job was going well, and she also had a job. Just before my twentieth birthday we found an apartment at Wellesley and Sherbourne Sts., which was close to work. We signed a one-year lease, but only intended to stay for the summer.

At the same time, I was seriously thinking of ending it with this guy that I was seeing. All we ever did, was go for drives and just have sex, and in his car too. I didn't mind the sex, but there was little conversation. When he did take me anywhere, it would be to introduce me to other men. I felt nervous at first, but as soon as they got affectionate, I melted in their arms. At home I wasn't treated like a loving child, but a burden. Deep down I knew that I was being used, but it felt so good and I just couldn't say no and hurt someone's feelings. *They wouldn't like me.*

One thing that sticks out in my mind was the day I did move out. I had all my personal belongings in a pile at the bottom of the stairs ready to go. Dad suddenly appears and asks me where I'm going. Without any explanation I told him I'm moving out, picked up my stuff and just left. *He had no idea what was going on at all.*

You Don't Remember– I can't Forget

My first time away from home was a summer I'll never forget; Cheyenne was living with her mother at the time that was only a few blocks away from me. We would go to hotels and get men to buy us drinks. I must admit, I was very nervous doing this. I just wanted to be liked and my curiosity always got the better of me. As soon as a guy showed me any affection, I couldn't say no.

I only partied on weekends. My job was always a priority with me and I never missed a day. Cheyenne and I hung out a lot and were like sisters, inseparable. I got hooked on cheap wine for a while, until I broke out in this awful rash. My roommate would get upset with me sometimes, because of my behavior. As the end of summer approached, my roommate started plotting ways to break the lease. I felt just awful, and a bit pissed off too. I talked to mom about the situation and she told me I could move back home. I had no other alternative.

The day I moved back home and got settled in, I found that no one questioned or said anything at all to me. I felt like I had done something wrong. Working was an escape from it all. As I said earlier, if I wasn't home, I would be visiting with my aunt or Cheyenne. *I wonder if I had been missed at all.*

During one visit with my aunt I told her that I didn't feel very good and that my stomach was bothering me. She suggested I go to this health clinic on Queen Street, near Broadview Avenue. On the day of the appointment I went on my own, and was worried just thinking about the white coat I would be seeing. I became really anxious and conjured up dreadful scenarios of being restrained. I was so nervous that I lost my trend of thought and forgot why I was there in the first place. I felt dreadful. When my name is called I'm taken to an examination room.

The white coat asked about my previous medical history. I told him what I knew about my accident and that I had a bone disease. Then he asked me about my last period. I felt embarrassed. What does that have to do with my stomachache? I told him that I've only had one period when I was sixteen and it only lasted two days. At that point his expression changed. He recommended that I see a specialist, a gynecologist, and proceeded to make all the arrangements for me. I had flashbacks of my very first internal examination at the hospital, when I was fifteen. What were these white coats looking for? I couldn't even discuss this issue with mom. Her character would change and she looked very uncomfortable. *What is wrong with me?*

I only missed a day of work and I was sitting in the living room watching television when my oldest brother came walking in with this girlfriend. They walked right past me and into the kitchen. He introduced her to mom and dad and then they left. My brother's actions hurt my feelings. He probably told her not to talk to me. *What is wrong with me?*

Over time, whenever possible, I did get a chance to speak to her. She was seven years younger than me; had three brothers and three sisters. She was also related to one of the girls I went to high school with, who was married by now. When her cousin found out that I was her boyfriend's sister she introduced me to her brother-in-law Geoff. He was charming and not bad looking and we started seeing each other. After a little over a month in the relationship he started talking a lot about getting married. In the back of my mind something didn't feel just right. Whenever we went out he never had any money and would be driving someone else's car. I was flattered, but reality sunk in. I couldn't have children, so I kept these feelings to myself and never discussed it with him. *(I had difficulty explaining my wants and needs to anyone).*

I've been at my job for four years now and everything was going well. Geoff called me at work one day and wanted to meet me and go out for lunch. We went to a drive thru restaurant and of course, I paid for lunch. When it was time for me to go back to work, he told me not to worry about it. *I can't remember what we did the rest of the afternoon, but I wasn't too happy about it.*

Of course, I didn't sleep well that night either, because I didn't get a chance to phone work and explain what happened. My mind was racing and wondering what I was going to do. There was no one to confide in. The next day, on my way to work, I just knew that I was in trouble, and kept telling myself that quitting, instead of getting fired, was probably the best thing to do. *I have difficultly sticking up for myself.*

My parents, especially dad, never gave me any tools for living. My body was sick, so therefore I probably wouldn't amount to anything of value. My first full time job lasted the longest, four years, while others lasted no more than two. It was a combination of self-confidence, limited patience and impulsivity. At least I could get Unemployment Insurance, so I handed in my resignation. I got a substantial severance pay, and then from out of nowhere dad started telling me that I should buy a house, because it's a good investment. I got very defensive. All of a sudden Geoff was showing an interest in my future! Having a house was a big responsibility and pressure, and I didn't think I could handle it. I bought a second hand car instead. I couldn't drive and gave it to him. We were a couple, right?

I decided to register with a personnel agency and work temporary for a while. I gained a lot of work experience by doing this, but was still leery of my co-workers. Eventually, the agency found me a full time position at a reputable jewelry company downtown. The position involved taking note of all the sales figures every month and balancing the books. When I wasn't busy, I would help out in other departments, so there was a lot of variety in this job.

I began having problems with Geoff. There were days when I didn't see or hear from him, and this really bothered me. When I saw mom I told her what is going on, she suggested that I call his mother. When his mom answered the phone, she started calling me, "a no good piece of shit, a slut, a tramp, etc." I couldn't believe what I was hearing and handed the phone to mom. She looked shocked, and hung up the phone. Then she walked over to one of the kitchen cupboards grabbed some sugar and poured it into a cup and then said, "C'mon."

We left the house and started walking up Pape and along Bain Avenue. I knew where we were going and now I was worried about a confrontation. When we got close to his mom's place I saw my car parked. We walked over to it and mom took off the gas cap, poured the whole cup of sugar down and without saying anything. We just walked backed home. Previous to that incident I had issues of betrayal and trust with my mother, and when I witnessed what she did for me that day I realized I had an ally.

The next day Geoff phoned me and started yelling and cursing at me. Wow, I couldn't believe it. The nerve of this guy, it's my car. A few days later someone broke into our house and my mother's purse was stolen. *I can't help blaming myself.*

Chapter 14

I kept the appointment with the Gynecologist and while I was in the waiting room I became very fearful. I conjured up dreadful scenarios of being restrained, lost my trend of thought and forgot why I was there in the first place. I felt horrible. When my name was called I entered the examination room.

The nurse told me to take all my clothes off, including underwear and gave me a gown to put on. I was lying on the bed and trying to stay calm down. Something awful was going to happen. I flashed back to my first internal examination, when I was fifteen years old and the humiliation I felt then came flooding back. When the nurse came back into the room, there were three male white coats with her; one of them did the internal examination; prodding and probing me, while the other one was examining my breasts. The conversation was only with the one white coat that was watching everything. He was the boss. I felt so mortified. What were they looking for? *What is wrong with me?*

I was put in the hospital on several occasions and underwent numerous tests, including eudiometrical biopsies. I was given the diagnosis of early menopause and then put on two types of medications. My periods were chemically induced, and I did not like that at all. These medications made me feel bloated; I'm a big girl and now I feel very uncomfortable and more self-conscious about my body than ever. After a three-month period of taking two types of pills I stopped, and felt better. I didn't miss having a period at all. However, not being able to conceive a child affected me more; I didn't feel whole. *There is no one to confide in either.*

The next day when I got to work the manager called me into his office. I was worried, what did I do now? I only took one day off. He tells me to take a seat and hands me a sales slip showing that I had purchased a wedding and engagement ring. I was absolutely shocked and speechless. Someone had forged my signature on this sales slip. The manager must have known that I had nothing to do with this, because of my reaction. Without a word he excused me and I just returned back to my desk, but in the back of my mind I knew who was responsible for this. *I am learning about vengeance.*

I did not know who to talk to or what to do about this situation and just went on with my life. I think my manager might have done something, because the Geoff ended up in Kingston Pen, without my intervention.

At home the atmosphere was always different. I never knew what to expect. On weekends when everyone was home and we didn't go for drives in the country, we would gather around the kitchen table and play cards. It was a lot of fun, until the criticizing started. It seemed that I didn't always play the right card, and the comments made me feel very unsure of myself. Of course, everyone said that they were just joking, but I felt embarrassed and thought about moving out again.

Most of the time my job was boring and it was a nice break to help out in other departments. I really didn't feel very comfortable with a lot of people that worked there, except this one girl Named Tanya. We got along really well. She was pregnant and would have to leave work soon. We both shared the same issues about our living arrangements, and talked about getting a place together. Eventually, we found a one-bedroom apartment in the Beaches area. I was so happy to be on my own again. When we got settled in we decided to have a house warming party and the strange thing was none of her family or friends came, just mine.

The party was just great and for quite some time besides drinking, I had been smoking pot and experimenting with other drugs. That night I took LSD for the first time and what a high. We had an old black and white television and all of a sudden everything was in color.

Everyone had a great time and from then on, my oldest brother started coming by more and more. I had mixed feelings about this. Deep down I hoped that our relationship could improve a lot. Then, one night he became verbally abusive with me; cursing at me to get lost, and go to my room. My roommate didn't do anything about the way he was talking to me either. I felt humiliated as I got to my room and didn't sleep well. He had a girlfriend. *I learn about deceit.*

I couldn't stand the way he was treating me and decided to tell mom. We were in the kitchen and I was telling her what was going on with my roommate and him. At that moment my brother's girlfriend and her friend walked into the kitchen. She demanded to know where my brother was and told us that she was pregnant. I was absolutely speechless. I knew exactly what he had been up to, but I didn't really know this girl. Sometimes she acted cold and distant towards me. My brother and I had a terrible relationship and I was sure these feelings he had for me spilled over into his personal life. *How do I tell her what's going on?*

When I returned home I told my roommate that my brother's girlfriend was pregnant. This information must have been devastating to her, because it wasn't long after our discussion that she had her baby. A boy. She must have gotten in touch with the baby's father, because in a couple of months we parted ways. I couldn't afford to live on my own and have no other recourse, but to move back home. *I try not to feel like a failure.*

Chapter 15

It was 1971 and in April was my brother's wedding. I felt sort of left out, because I was not involved in the wedding party or any preparation at all. I did go to the Wedding Showers though and enjoyed myself. My brother, John and I did not have a very positive relationship, as he was always trying to discredit me, which did affect the relationship with my sister-in-law. The Church was located in the Beaches and just beautiful (Describe the church a bit). Denise looked just beautiful as she walked down the aisle. She wore a wedding gown even though she was three months pregnant, and some of the guests made comments about that. The Reception was at our house and it turned out to be good day.

In October, my sister-in-law went into labor, however, both she and the baby were in distress. When mom and I got to the hospital I was really worried. Only the parents could go in and see her. When mom came back to the waiting area she told me she had a boy. I was so worried, almost in a panic, and asked her if the baby will get sick like me. She reassured me that they were both doing fine and I was relieved. I'm an aunt, but the relationship that my brother and I had interfered with this aspect too.

Work was going well, and I started to feel antsy about my job. I was starting to sense indifference from the other employees. They were not very talkative or friendly and I couldn't help feeling that there was something wrong with me. I've been at this job for almost two and a half years and still couldn't balance the books. I was getting bored and frustrated with the whole scene. Then I met this guy, who worked in a different department. It made going to work worthwhile. We got along well and I invited him over to my place a few times. The only place to have any privacy was my room and I confided to him that I smoked pot and when I asked him if he wanted to share a joint with me he said no, and that was that. It was nice to feel that somebody cared and I looked forward to seeing him at work.

One morning as soon as I sat at my desk the manager called me into his office. The assistant manager was there too. He motioned me to take a seat and to my complete surprise and shock he started giving me a lecture about the dangers of smoking pot and doing drugs. I was speechless. Oh, I could hear him all right, but all I can think about was this guy who ratted on me. They didn't fire me, but laid me off, which was good, because I could collect Unemployment Insurance. I felt so betrayed by this coworker. This only made me smoke pot, and drink more to cover up my true feelings. During this hiatus from work I had a lot of scary moments; a date rape and nasty threatening phone calls from other men I was seeing. *There's no one I could confide in either.*

I had no ambition and would mope around the house, spending most of the time in my room, especially when dad was home. I felt depressed; my confidence was really low and I just didn't know what to do with my life. Mom encouraged me to look for another job; and suggested that the employment office might help. I thought about what she said and took her advice. Feelings of desperation set in, having no money and wanting to leave home was the catalyst. I registered with a few Personnel Agencies again, and the temporary jobs were interesting, and a good working experience.

The seventies and in my twenties was a troubling time for me. I just couldn't get interested in anything for too long. My downfall was being disillusioned by people and easily distracted too much by their negativity. Subconsciously, I was pushing people away and whenever there was a roadblock, or an upset, I would eat. I was afraid of authority, and hesitant to ask for help in sticking up for myself during a crisis. I was between jobs at the time, living at home and feeling miserable. My oldest brother asked me if I could move in for a while. My nephew was three years old now and my sister-in-law was pregnant again. She needed help around the house and he offered to pay me ten dollars a week. I said yes and we began to get along. I really appreciated what my brother did for me then. It meant a lot to me, but I never told him so.

I enjoyed looking after my nephew, but couldn't get close to my sister-in-law. In November of '74 she had a healthy baby boy. They started looking for larger accommodations and I ended up moving back home. I started going on interviews and found work at a Custom Brokers downtown doing Accounts Receivable/Payables and after a few months of working, I started thinking of moving out again. There was a rooming house that you could see from the back of our house. The front room on the second floor was for rent and I took it. I had a hot plate with two burners and had to wash my dishes in the bathtub. It was a difficult adjustment, because I'm on my own, no roommate. I felt really alone and home sick.

Whenever I went home, which was often, mom would answer the door, and ask, "What are you doing here?" Her comment did bother me somewhat, but I just couldn't stay away. Working and keeping busy helped. I did not like weekends. I had feelings of abandonment and rejection; no one came to visit. *What is wrong with me?*

My aunt volunteered at a Community Center and asked me if I would like to get involved. I was glad that I did, because it involved working with a team of people who arranged dances and other events. We would all take turns working the door, selling tickets, doing bartending, and looking after coats and belongings. I made up flyers and learned how to do silk screening. It was a great learning experience for me, especially working the door and having a bit of authority.

When the dance started, and I was on a break, I sat with other volunteers or family, but always in the corner hoping no one would ask me to dance. When a guy did approach me for a dance, my character changed completely. I did comply, because I wanted to be liked, but felt very self-conscious, like everyone s watching me. My encounters with the opposite sex were not a positive thing. I didn't feel attractive at all and figured their only motive was to have sex. *I think that's all I'm good for!*

My job was just great; I trained new staff for reception work, learned to use a Dictaphone, telex machine, etc., and eventually I was promoted to Executive Secretary. I was very proud of my accomplishments and then after three and half years the company decided to change the payroll to once a month and I quit.

I didn't have another job to go to and got into a slump, because of my financial situation, I had to move back home. Mom didn't seem to mind, but dad started his criticisms toward me. *I'm not a failure.*

Mom keeps telling me he is joking. I think about moving out. Dad is drinking more and his demeanor has changed. Mom confided in me that she is even afraid of him sometimes.

I registered with a personnel agency, and they found me a temporary job at an insurance company downtown. There wasn't much variety just a lot of typing. I must have done a good job, because after three months they wanted to hire me. I said yes.

At home nothing much changed. My brothers were working with dad now and learning the renovation business, and it was going well. Mom typed up invoices and receipts for them, so they could get paid. Watching her type was funny, because she only used one finger.

Then the unexpected happened. My room was close to the bathroom and around midnight, I heard a loud thump in the hall. I got up to investigate and I saw mom lying on the bathroom floor. Oh my God, I screamed as I ran down the stairs and out the front door looking for help. I heard dad behind me yelling at me to get back into the house and shut up. I went right up to my room and lay on my bed worried about mom as I heard the ambulance take her away. I did have to go to work the next day, and it was difficult to sleep. My bedroom was always warm, and when I finally fell asleep I started to experience these unbelievable chills. I wasn't scared at all as I lay in the dark shivering and hugging my blankets. *I know it is mom, and she is in distress.*

In the morning I was so exhausted that I didn't go to work. I called my aunt and we went to see mom. I was shaken when I saw her. She had a full Hysterectomy. I never thought I'd be visiting my mother in the hospital. She acted like everything was fine and not to worry, but I was.

It was a relief when she was able to leave the hospital and come home. Dad was always working and not much support. Of course, she had to take it easy and I was glad to be there for her. Dad asked me to type up the invoices and I couldn't say no.
I was very particular with detail, and did a great job, because it was my profession. I felt insulted though because after I typed up an invoice dad threw a twenty-dollar bill at me.

I started having these awful dreams. Dad is standing at the top of the stairs. I sneak up behind him and push him. He is lying at the bottom of the stairs dead. I would wake up in a sweat and shake it off. Every night for at least a week the dreams continued.

I've been working for this company about six months now and I found it hard to concentrate, because of the issues at home. My sleep was interrupted. I had been getting into trouble at work and not meeting their expectations. I told my supervisor what was going on at home. She sympathized with me, and the pressure eased off somewhat.

There was no one who I could confide in and it was very difficult for me to ask for help and these dreams were very disturbing to me. I made an appointment to see a white coat. My mind was racing. I felt nervous and scared as the nurse took me to the examination room. As soon as I sat down in the white coats office and try to explain my problems I broke down and cried uncontrollably. She handed me a box of Kleenex and patiently waited for me to continue. When I told her about my dad's attitude and these dreams I was having, I felt better. The end result was that I should move out. She suggested I check in with some housing connections and offered to write a note that would help speed up the process. The envelope wasn't sealed so I read it and it stated that I was emotionally unstable. *Oh my God, what is wrong with me!*

There was no way that I was going to show this letter to anyone and tore it up. I remembered that the corner store had a one-bedroom apartment for rent. Before I walked into the house I went to inquire about it, and spoke to the owner. It was located above a store at Queen and Morse streets. It was a nice set up, very roomy and I could afford to pay the rent. I had a flight of stairs to contend with, but I still took it. My brothers helped me move in, which I really appreciated. I was alone again, so I got a cat for company and felt good about my life. I was not dating anyone per say, but my emotional needs were being met. I got really good at manipulating men for my sexual needs.

Chapter16

My two youngest brothers still lived at home. I didn't see the older ones that much and when I saw mom, she still didn't look one hundred percent. She showed me a nasty looking sore on her neck that just wouldn't go away. She had an appointment coming up to have a biopsy done on it. The results were devastating. She was diagnosed with terminal lung cancer.

No one wanted to believe it and questioned why or how this could happen. This was the worst time of my life, because I was living on my own and had no one to share my feelings with. Mom was staying at my oldest brother's place and I just didn't or couldn't understand why. They only had two bedrooms, two young boys and Denise was pregnant with her third child.

Mom was moved to different hospitals for different treatments, as her condition worsened. Sometimes I got upset with the white coats. Whenever she had surgery, I would experience unbelievable chills throughout my body. I was very worried about her and didn't function well. My work was suffering, because I missed a lot of days.

I still volunteered at the community center every Friday night and when there was a dance and it was very emotional. Everyone was having such a great time while my mother was dying. I've been up to my brothers a few times to see mom, but the atmosphere there was not good. Of course, there was a lot of tension in the air. My sister-in-law was pregnant and there must have been a lot of demands on her. When my brother asked me to baby sit, I said yes. They really needed a break and it was nice spending time with mom. They didn't say where or when they would be home. Mom was on the couch not looking too well and the boys were in bed asleep. I made tea for us and it was like old times. I could tell she was in a lot of pain. She really hated dad for abandoning her when she needed him the most, and was upset that she was not in her own home. She was worried about the grandchildren and her youngest son, who was now seventeen. She got so much off her chest and the hardest thing for me was that I had to promise her that I wouldn’t say anything. While she was sick her stepfather died. It was best that we didn’t tell her this and it was hard for me not to tell her.

When my brother and his wife got home I was not too pleased. It was really late and I had to go to work the next day. I called a taxi and on the way home I felt terrible for some of the things I said to them. *It is a terrible time for everyone really, watching someone die and there’s nothing you can do.*

A couple of days went by, when I got a call from the hospital; her condition has taken a turn for the worse. On the way to the hospital I was in a panic. When I saw her I was shocked, but stayed as composed as I could. She was in so much pain and gasping for air that she could only able to speak in a whisper. “Why me, why me?” I have seen death stare at me; eyes that have a certain longing, but no feeling; a body dealing with death, but a mind fighting not to believe that this could really happen. My second oldest brother came into the room, but we didn’t say much to each other. It was such an emotional time. I tried to comfort my mom by rubbing her chest and she motioned me to come closer. She asked me to get in touch with a friend of hers.

My brother and I had a hard time leaving her there. When I got home I called her closest friend and told her that mom wanted to see her. The very next day her friend went and visited with her and later that night, mom died. She was only forty-eight years old. I was thirty-one years of age and experienced such aloneness. The only person, who really cared about me, was gone forever.

My oldest brother and I made the arrangements for her funeral. Dad’s wishes were that she be cremated, which bothered me, but I had no say in the matter. My oldest brother was the boss when dad was not around and there just didn’t seem to be any sentiment at all.

I had a little breakdown and ended up at my aunt’s house. She gave me a nerve pill, which calmed me down. One of my cousins stayed with me for a few days and when I went back to work; without any compassion I was fired on the spot.

I applied for Unemployment Insurance and was turned down. I then tried Welfare. Same thing. My financial situation was getting worse and I was feeling very desperate. I had to do something, or I'd end up on the street, homeless. Dad had lots of room and I had nowhere else to go. There was only one brother living at home now, with whom I got along with pretty well. When I got up enough nerve to ask him I was relieved that he said yes. I was shocked when he put a mattress in a corner of the dining room, by a window, for there was where I was to sleep. I felt humiliated, and depressed, but had no other options at the time. *He shows me no compassion at all and I start having terrible dreams about him again.*

I still volunteered at the center, which helped with my grieving, along with drinking and drugs. On some occasions I would see my aunt there. She never judged me and I thought maybe she could help me out. One of my brothers stayed in her attic once, but it was empty now and I was desperate, so I got up enough nerve to ask her if I could stay there. She said yes. *God bless her.*

The stairs scared me, because they were steep. There were two small rooms adjacent to each other, with a small landing dividing both. The walls were a dingy yellow; probably due to cigarette smoke. The window, facing the main street, almost covered the entire wall, but needed to be cleaned. The sitting room, had old furniture scattered about, including an old trunk that doubled as a coffee table, but it was my sitting room. The other room had a small cot and a dresser and was quite roomy and comfortable. There was one large window, which also covered the wall and opened up and led out onto the roof. This was cool. I only slept up there and spent a lot of time with my aunt and cousins.

When I got settled in I started thinking about going back to work, but I lacked the confidence. I just didn't know what to do until my aunt suggested that I speak to a doctor about my concerns. Oh boy, right away I thought about the note and the comment 'emotionally disturbed', from the last white coat I confided in. I felt nervous but didn't know what else to do about my situation.

It didn't take long to get an appointment, and while I was sitting in the waiting room, feeling anxious and nervous, while trying to stay focused about what I need. *This is a crisis. I have to get on with my life. Nobody cares about me.*

The nurse took me to an examination room and my mind started to race. When the white coat came and sat across from me she asked me what was wrong. I tried to explain my dilemma and broke down, crying uncontrollably. She handed me a box of Kleenex, and when I calmed down and explained my situation, she offered me some good advice. Because I had a spinal cord injury, I might be eligible to attend a workshop for physically disabled adults, which would help me get back into the workforce. She helped me fill out the application, especially the medical questions. I was feeling a little apprehensive because I thought it was like school, until I took a tour of the facility.

Chapter 17

I was thrilled when I got a letter stating that I was eligible for the program. Some of the clientele are around my own age with different forms of disability, which I had no difficulty getting along with. I thought about my time spent in the hospital, and even though I was still leery of people, this would be a turning point in my life. *I miss mom.* .

This facility was a workshop for people with various disabilities who were assigned to different workstations in order to find out what type of job they were best suited for. There were all types of workstations, conveyor belts with assembly lines, a machine that sealed a product in plastic and even an office setting, with typing and where I learned how to do payroll.

At first you were assessed on numerous tasks; conveyor belt, packaging and stacking shelves, etc. There was also group therapy. It took me some time to get used to the counselor; she reminded me of a white coat. She did help me come to terms with some things that I was carrying around from my past. After completing all the workstations I ended up in the office doing typing and payroll, which I enjoyed. I still volunteered at the community center too. Halloween was coming and the group met at one of the member's homes, to discuss about having a dance. During the meeting I couldn't keep my eyes off of this one guy, who I've worked with many times. I could feel an unexplainable pulling towards him. The spokesperson that was running the meeting must have noticed something between us. When the meeting was over he asked this guy to walk me home. I was still living at my aunts and the walk home was very pleasant. The weather was just great, mild and there were a few stars in the sky. We discussed the upcoming dance. I felt so comfortable with him. We said goodnight, and made arrangements to meet again for coffee another day.

You Don't Remember– I can't Forget

There was a coffee shop at the end of my street and I was surprised when Gino called and asked me to meet him. I was happy when he did show up. We weren't complete strangers, because when I decided to volunteer at the center, I found out that he had been there for quite some time. He knew that I drank and did drugs, because other volunteers did too, but he didn't get involved.

I did have a difficult time relating my feelings to anyone, especially the opposite sex, but Gino was different. Even though there were times when he was lost In thought, we was always polite, a real gentleman, something I've never experienced, but it felt good. I told him what I was going through; losing my mother and then my job; and because I have a spinal cord injury that I was attending a workshop. It surprised me when he told me that he attended the same workshop, but didn't like it. *This workshop is not specifically suited for people with acquired brain injuries.*

He was dealing with a lot also, recovering from the after affects of a lengthy illness called, Encephalitis (an acquired brain injury) and Epilepsy, which I didn't know anything about them at the time. He recently lost his father too and felt that his family didn't understand him. We had a lot in common. Dealing with the reality of how friends and family's attitudes change when suddenly struck down with a lengthy illness. The more time we spent together, the more I began losing interest in the Workshop, it was getting boring. I started taking Fridays off and we would get together, including most weekends. Of course, I would get a lecture when I went back to the workshop. He was also starting to get flack from his family. Eventually the workshop found me a job at an organization that helps people with disabilities get back into the workforce. I was a secretary in the Rehabilitation Department, typing up reports from counselors who were personally involved in their progress. I enjoyed going to seminars that identified specific traits that related to physical and intellectual disabilities. Eventually, I started to train some of these clients, young and old, to do reception work. It was very rewarding work and such a learning experience, especially when the client obtained employment.

When I introduced my boyfriend to dad and my brothers, Gino was in disbelief as to the way they treated me, especially my oldest brother. He was instrumental in helping me become objective to my spirit. When he was not around they made derogatory remarks regarding his character. When I met his family, I felt such apathy towards him, because they had no patience for him. They never let him finish a sentence. His mother's English was very limited so communication between her and I was not good. It was the winter of 1954 when his parents along with three brothers and two sisters arrived here from Italy. Gino was born two years later. I believe that things happen for a reason, and that we were brought together via the death of his father and my mother. Despite a lot of adversity from both families, together we had overcome the negative, but that's another story.

The End

Epilog

I could never discern why the rapport between doctors and me was so negative. This stigma followed me throughout my adulthood. Whenever I see a white coat I become very nervous, lose my trend of thought and forget why I am here in the first place. They have misdiagnosed me as being emotionally unstable or high strung.

One day I was explaining to a coworker the issues I had whenever I had to see a doctor. Well, unbeknownst to me, both her parents are medical professionals. Right away she said to me. "You have White Coat Syndrome." She explained the symptoms a little bit. Wow, it made sense; however, I was not sure where this dilemma originated.

At the same time I've been seeing a white coat on a consistent basis, and of course, whenever I see her I feel negative and anxious to begin with. She keeps insisting that I am suffering from depression, and started prescribing psychotropic drugs for this. This medication made me feel like a zombie, and was affecting my day-to-day activities. Especially my job. I would try to tell the white coat how these drugs made me feel and all she did was prescribe a different drug. This went on for months and then she suggested I see a psychiatrist. The thought of seeing a psychiatrist depressed me, at first. I'm not crazy! These drugs the white coat was prescribing were not helping me at all, so if seeing a psychiatrist seemed to be the only alternative to this dilemma, then I agreed.

The psychiatrist's office was located in a building next to a different hospital. Her office was to be found in the basement, down a long narrow hallway with numerous doors on either side. I felting very nervous when I finally found the door and knocked.

As I entered, there was no bed in the room, but shelves with lots of books on them. I sat in a nice comfortable chair facing her and the conversation was geared more towards my emotional needs and wants. After two and half hours she concluded that my depression was a result of the physical pain I was experiencing. She would inform my doctor of this, including details regarding medication. When I brought up the issue of White Coat Syndrome, she suggested that I discuss this with the doctor.

After that meeting I stopped taking all the medication, except for hormone replacement and the blood pressure pill. During my next visit with the white coat, I informed her what the psychiatrist told me about my depression and that she would be sending her a detailed report. Now comes the hard part. I informed her that I suffer from white coat syndrome. Her immediate response is, 'children get that'! Her reply is profound. I immediately caught my breath, my mouth opened as if to scream, and my childhood flashed in front of me. It happened so fast too. That terrified little girl, unable to move and surrounded by people in white coats; all these years traumatized by past events. Wow!

Her comments were a turning point in my life (a light bulb moment). The feeling was very surreal; I was not that little girl anymore, but an adult, and had the right to be in control.

From that moment on I realized how a trauma from the past could imprison our minds. The anxiety is still with me, but has lessened somewhat. I don't think it will ever go away, but just being able to acknowledge my dilemma with a doctor is wonderful. They would offer to take off their white coats, which helps me calm down and justify my health concerns in a more positive frame of mind.

Author's Note

Is our birth and growth into adulthood an experience or experiment? I was born sick, but nobody suspected a thing until an accident that crippled me and saved my life. What an oxymoron! I was given a second chance at life, but why were people trying to crush my spirit, my essence?

The effects of emotional negligence, issues of abandonment, betrayal, isolation and rejection led to feelings of low self esteem, which resulted in drug and alcohol abuse; the desolation of the human spirit. I am a survivor, and Adversity is my middle name.

Names and dates are irrelevant and to blame anyone specifically is not the issue here. My story is one of cause and effect, a voyage in some ways, of events that still disturb me, somewhat. A sense of belonging, in the form of bonding, depression, (physical pain), betrayal; White Coat Syndrome and most of all, being misunderstood (indifference).

I strongly believe that the hardships (experiences) that we face in life are a testament (experiment) to our future. If we choose not to accept our suffering (hardships) we will never know bliss. Such is the root of violence. Today, in the millennium, the words abuse and dysfunction are spoken too flippantly. We live in an age, which flatters itself that it can find a remedy to almost every problem it, creates. Why is there so much neglect and negative aggression? Is the justification for this behavior a result of indifference?

Afterthought

Writing this book I have overcome a lot of obstacles; barriers that unhappy people tried to belittle my mind with. I understood blame and guilt before anything else and was surrounded by narcissists.

You don't remember, because you've never walked in my shoes. I can't forget, but with hard work and determination, I can repudiate my past.

Acknowledgements

This book is dedicated to numerous people who helped me face life's objectives.

To my mother, who had such strength and fortitude; she encouraged me to never give up and taught me how to be resourceful.

To my father, who was a hard working person. He discouraged me and yet through his negative actions I learned so much about the dark side of human nature.

To numerous people in the business community, who recognized my potential, and gave me the opportunity to flourish.

Most importantly to my husband, who gives me a sense of well being, shows me respect and most of all taught me to love myself.

Thank you Doug Baker for introducing us.

LaVergne, TN USA
30 August 2010
195177LV00001B/180/P

9 780980 907506